Your
Horoscope
2021

....

Scorpio

24 October – 22 November

igloobooks

igloobooks

Published in 2020
by Igloo Books Ltd
Cottage Farm
Sywell
NN6 0BJ
www.igloobooks.com

Copyright © 2019 Igloo Books Ltd
Igloo Books is an imprint of Bonnier Books UK

0820 001
2 4 6 8 10 9 7 5 3 1
ISBN 978-1-83852-325-1

Written by Belinda Campbell and Denise Evans

Cover design by Simon Parker
Edited by Bobby Newlyn-Jones

Printed and manufactured in China

CONTENTS

. . . .

INTRODUCTION
· · · · · · · · · · · · · · · · ·

This 15-month guide has been designed and written to give
a concise and accessible insight into both the nature of your
star sign and the year ahead. Divided into two main sections,
the first section of this guide will give you an overview of your
character in order to help you understand how you think,
perceive the world and interact with others and – perhaps just
as importantly – why. You'll soon see that your zodiac sign
is not just affected by a few stars in the sky, but by planets,
elements, and a whole host of other factors, too.

The second section of this guide is made up of daily forecasts.
Use these to increase your awareness of what might appear on
your horizon so that you're better equipped to deal with the
days ahead. While this should never be used to dictate your
life, it can be useful to see how your energies might be affected
or influenced, which in turn can help you prepare for what life
might throw your way.

By the end of these 15 months, these two sections should
have given you a deeper understanding and awareness of
yourself and, in turn, the world around you. There are never
any definite certainties, but with an open mind you will find
guidance for what might be, and learn to take more control of
your own destiny.

THE CHARACTER OF
THE SCORPION
··················

Highly intimate, transformative, and controlled, Scorpios are the seducers of the zodiac calendar that are hard to resist. Whilst the affection of a Scorpio can be addictive, their passion can quickly feel possessive, so don't enter a serious relationship with this intense sign lightly. If you get on the wrong side of this powerful sign, whether it's by hurting them or someone that they fiercely love, then prepare yourself for an almighty sting from this Scorpion's tail; just as their love is unforgettable, so is their scorn. Associated with the genitals, Scorpios may struggle to separate themselves from their sexy reputation, however private they keep their love lives.

Scorpios are perhaps the deepest of all the water signs and so can require some extra patience and searching to get to the core of their mysterious self. Scorpios have a negative energy that means that most of their emotions will be kept internal, however, they might like to express their emotions through writing, like Scorpio poet and novelist, Sylvia Plath. This sign doesn't like to allow itself to be vulnerable, (remember their rather sensitive associated part of the body), so trust and loyalty may be hard won. This Scorpion is quick to protect themselves and their loved ones from any harm so may keep their armour up until they decide it's safe to let someone in.

Born in the middle of autumn, Scorpio is a fixed sign that may enjoy security and can be single-minded in their approach towards reaching their goals. Co-ruled by Mars and Pluto, these astrological bodies give Scorpios a controlled and competitive attitude that will generally mean that they end up getting what they want out of life once they set their mind to it; take the three Scorpio Jenners, Kendall, Kris, and Caitlyn, as perfect examples of Scorpio's sexiness, controlling nature, and ability to transform.

THE SCORPION

Terrifying for most people to behold, the venom in their tail perhaps not helping, the Scorpion has a fierce reputation that some Scorpios can most certainly live up to, however, there is so much more to this creature than just their sting. Throughout a scorpion's life, it will shed its exoskeleton when it becomes too small and emerge larger and more powerful than before. Scorpios may experience a similar transformation within their lifetime, whether it's shedding their childhood as they move away to university, deciding on a change in career in their later years, or an internal transformation of some kind. Whilst the scorpion and Scorpio go through these changes they can be at their most vulnerable as their new-found selves fully form. However, once the transformation is complete both will reveal themselves stronger and more powerful than before. The scorpion is a predatory and defensive creature. Just like a Scorpio, they can go after what they want and are prone to lash out if they feel confronted. A nocturnal animal, Scorpios may also enjoy plenty of partying on nights out in their younger years; find them in the clubs shining under the ultraviolet lights like the mysteriously glowing scorpion!

PLUTO AND MARS

Renamed a dwarf planet in 2006, Pluto co-rules the sign of Scorpio with Mars. Pluto's demotion has made it no less mysterious to onlookers and its secrets are yet to be fully understood, which makes it a fitting ruler for the secretive Scorpio. Named after the Roman God of the Underworld, this planet is associated with power and depth, just like the emotionally deep and controlling sign of Scorpio. The measured power from Pluto teamed with Scorpio's other ruling planet, Mars, makes for a sign that has controlled energy with plenty of drive and fight. Named after the Greek God of War, Mars is linked with passion and can feed into a Scorpio's possessive and sensuous nature. From Mars, Scorpios can find the courage to go after what they desire, both in their personal and professional lives. Born in the eighth house in the zodiac calendar, which is associated with regeneration, the power of Pluto and the strength of Mars means that Scorpios can hold huge potential for transformation and may choose to reinvent themselves several times over.

ELEMENTS, MODES AND POLARITIES

Each sign is made up of a unique combination of three defining groups: elements, modes and polarities. Each of these defining parts can manifest themselves in good and bad ways and none should be seen to be a positive or a negative – including the polarities! Just like a jigsaw puzzle, piecing these groups together can help illuminate why each sign has certain characteristics and help us find a balance.

ELEMENTS

Fire: Dynamic and adventurous, signs with fire in them can be extroverted. Others are naturally drawn to them because of the positive light they give off, as well as their high levels of energy and confidence.

Earth: Signs with the earth element are steady and driven with their ambitions. They make for a solid friend, parent or partner due to their grounded influence and nurturing nature.

Air: The invisible element that influences each of the other elements significantly, air signs will provide much-needed perspective to others with their fair thinking, verbal skills and key ideas.

Water: Warm in the shallows and freezing as ice. This mysterious element is essential to the growth of everything around it, through its emotional depth and empathy.

MODES

Cardinal: Pioneers of the calendar, cardinal signs jump-start each season and are the energetic go-getters.

Fixed: Marking the middle of the calendar, fixed signs firmly denote and value steadiness and reliability.

Mutable: As the seasons end, the mutable signs adapt and give themselves over gladly to the promise of change.

POLARITIES

Positive: Typically extroverted, positive signs take physical action and embrace outside stimulus in their life.

Negative: Usually introverted, negative signs value emotional development and experiencing life from the inside out.

SCORPIO IN BRIEF

The table below shows the key attributes of Scorpio.
Use it for quick reference and to understand more about this fascinating sign.

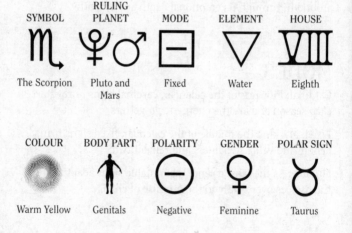

SYMBOL	RULING PLANET	MODE	ELEMENT	HOUSE
The Scorpion	Pluto and Mars	Fixed	Water	Eighth

COLOUR	BODY PART	POLARITY	GENDER	POLAR SIGN
Warm Yellow	Genitals	Negative	Feminine	Taurus

ROMANTIC RELATIONSHIPS

. . . .

When it comes to Scorpio's relationships, there is no dipping your toe in with this water sign, their love is more like plunging head first from the highest diving board. The intensity of sexpot Scorpio's affection can be scary for some and less-daring signs may feel intimidated by their passion, but those that are brave enough to take the plunge will be rewarded with Scorpio's exhilarating and all-consuming love. A Scorpio might have their partners jump through some hoops to test their loyalty, but it's only to see if they are as serious about the relationship as the Scorpio is; only then will Scorpios really open up to their partners. When Scorpios fall in love it is truly, madly and deeply with their heart, body and soul.

In a long-term relationship, this fixed sign can have a steadfast approach to the one they love; there's nothing fickle about Scorpio's feelings. A committed Scorpio is loyal and protective and will always come to their partner's defence. Potential partners will be attracted to sexy Scorpio's charisma and enigmatic charm, but only the lucky ones will know Scorpio's deepest secrets and feelings as this secretive sign will only share these with a chosen few in their lifetime. Once a Scorpio lays claim to their chosen partner, their passionate love can turn into an obsessive jealousy if they're not careful.

With the influence of Pluto, Scorpios may experience some power struggles in their relationships and with their warring planet of Mars guiding them, disagreements can turn into a battlefield if emotions run high. Possessive Scorpios should try to resist controlling their partner and give them as much autonomy in the relationship as necessary, especially with individualist and free-spirited signs like Aquarius and Sagittarius. Regardless of what has set Scorpio to attack mode, if a Scorpion is arguing with their lover it is because they think they are worth fighting for. If you are an angered Scorpio or fighting with one, try to turn that intensity into passion rather than rage.

ARIES: COMPATIBILITY 2/5

If it's passion Aries desires in a relationship, a Scorpio could be the perfect sign for romance. However, this match might be too controlling and combative for long-term happiness. Both ruled by the planet Mars, these two may come into this relationship armed and ready to fight. Scorpio's controlling and jealous tendencies could be a source of many of these steaming fights with this water sign. If this fire and water duo can work out a balance of control and ease the Scorpio lover's jealousy, then these two could have one steamy relationship rather than being left hot and bothered.

TAURUS: COMPATIBILITY 5/5

Scorpio and Taurus are each other's opposites on the zodiac calendar so cosmically share a special relationship both in their differences and similarities. The element of Taurus is earth and Scorpio's water which usually will mean that both partners will provide something that the other desperately needs. Love and passion are both driving forces for these two. Scorpio has the reputation for being the sexiest of signs and Taurus the most beautiful, so a physical relationship should be strong here. Whilst this couple will no doubt enjoy each other's bodies, their tendencies towards possession and jealousy will need to be kept in check.

GEMINI: COMPATIBILITY 3/5

Passionate debates could be on the menu for a Scorpio and Gemini love affair. The water sign of Scorpio will bring emotional depth to the relationship whilst a Gemini's air influence will help breathe a fresh perspective on things. Scorpios risk suffocating Geminis with their intense emotions if turned toxic. Geminis can be flirtatious which can trigger Scorpio's jealousy, but Geminis aren't scared of a little arguing, in fact they quite like the stimulation. Being a fixed sign, Scorpios value steadiness so may find flighty Gemini too unreliable, however, this relationship has the potential to be full of spice and interest.

CANCER: COMPATIBILITY 2/5

These two water signs can easily get lost in each other's emotions. Ruled by Mars, Scorpio's passion for their Cancerian lover will be intense and a Cancerian will likely be highly attracted to a sensual Scorpio. Both the Scorpion and Crab can be stubborn and unwilling to bend to their partner's wishes if they don't match their own. Claws and stingers at the ready, disagreements could see both sides getting hurt and might end with them parting ways quickly. However, once these two decide that they want to be together, they can experience a love that is unfailing in its loyalty.

LEO: COMPATIBILITY 1/5

The love between water sign Scorpio and fiery Leo can be one of deep intimacy or dampened spirits. Here are two fixed signs that could clash in their different approaches and refuse to yield to each other's strong personalities. Shared assets, particularly money, could prove difficult for a Scorpio and Leo. Scorpio is born in the eighth house where shared possessions are important, and Leos belong in the fourth house where a love of gambling lives which could result in conflict for the couple. If respect is exercised regularly between these two lovers, theirs is a closeness well worth protecting.

VIRGO: COMPATIBILITY 5/5

Placed two apart on the zodiac calendar, the passionate and loyal bond between the Virgin and Scorpion is a special one. Orderly Virgos will value the steadiness of a fixed sign Scorpio, and similarly the loyal Scorpio will appreciate the faithfulness that many Virgos are known for. With their complimentary elements of water and earth and their matching negative energies, this typically introvert couple will enjoy the nourishing effects of spending quality time with each other. Theirs is an intimate relationship but not without some passionate arguments thanks to power ruled Scorpio's influence of Pluto and Virgo's sharp tongue.

LIBRA: COMPATIBILITY 2/5

When the planets align for Scorpio and Libra, the combination of loving Venus, passionate Mars, and powerful Pluto can make for an intimate and stimulating love affair. The emotions of a water sign and mindfulness of air can be a harmonious pairing so long as a Scorpio and Libra are on the same page. Libras can feel superficial to the deep feeling Scorpio, but thankfully when this head and heart ruled couple fail to understand each other, Libra's charm and diplomacy can help calm any troubled waters. This love won't be without conflicts, sorry Libra, but it could be loyal and long-lasting.

SCORPIO: COMPATIBILITY 4/5

Was there ever a couple more deeply and desperately devoted to one another than Scorpio and Scorpio? The intimate connection that these two mysterious introverts can make is both in mind and body. They both can be guilty of passionate outbursts, particularly with jealousy, and their fixed attitudes can lead to arguments if they can't agree. If these two can patiently hold their breath in stormier times then this is a relationship that could sail off into the sunset together. Scorpio and Scorpio are a true power couple that thanks to their hardy Scorpion nature can withstand plenty.

SAGITTARIUS: COMPATIBILITY 2/5

Sagittarius and Scorpio can have a daring partnership; whether their gamble on each other pays off is another thing entirely. The adventurous Sagittarian will help expand Scorpio's horizons and appeal to their brave side, whilst Scorpio's fixed attitude can teach the flaky Sagittarian to stay motivated and see things through. The love of Scorpio can be all encompassing and the worst thing for a Sagittarian is for them to feel like their partner is at all possessive. This is definitely not a boring love, but flexibility and growth are both key for these two getting the most out of the relationship.

CAPRICORN: COMPATIBILITY 5/5

When Capricorn and Scorpio set their sights on each other, these highly dedicated signs could be in it for the long run. Placed two apart on the Zodiac calendar, theirs is a devout bond that is likely to be highly compatible with matching negative energies, complementary elements, and harmonising cardinal and fixed modes. A Capricorn can offer the security that Scorpio desires and Scorpio can be the powerful influence that feeds Capricorn's ambition. Scorpio will bring the fun and Capricorn will bring the itinerary to go with it. If they can take it in turns to rule the roost, their love could go the distance.

AQUARIUS: COMPATIBILITY 1/5

Mysterious Scorpio and unique Aquarius may well find themselves attracted to one another, but the Scorpion and Water Bearer may need to work hard to keep their relationship off the rocks. Positive Aquarians are outgoing, and socialising in their communities is important, but this contrasts with introverted Scorpios who tend to have a small and intimate circle of friends. Their modes are both fixed which means they can be resistant to changing their contrasting outlooks. If stable Scorpio can embrace this air sign's free-spirited nature and rational Aquarius can provide the intimacy that Scorpio needs, then these two could find their happiness.

PISCES: COMPATIBILITY 4/5

Here are two water signs that will go to the ends of the Earth, or rather the depths of the oceans for one another. Pisceans dream of finding that fantasy love and the enigmatic Scorpio can be just that for them, whilst the empathetic Pisces can be the kindred spirit that secretive Scorpios can finally be vulnerable with. A Piscean's mutable nature, that flows with change can be at odds with the steadfast approach of a fixed Scorpio, but their differences mean that they have plenty to learn from each other. Emotional security and sensitivity are where these two thrive.

FAMILY AND FRIENDS

. . . .

The negative energy in Scorpios means that this sign is quite happy to spend time alone, however, even if they do not actively seek out new friendships, the bonds that this sign will make are extremely important to them. Scorpio's group of friends is likely to be small as they value quality over quantity. Each friend of a Scorpio will have been carefully selected and may have gone through vigorous tests set by their Scorpion comrade to prove their worthiness. The reason for Scorpio's caginess comes back to their fear of letting their guard down and exposing themselves to pain; trust is an important practice for any Scorpio who wants to experience the benefits of close friendship.

As with most relationships, whether it be friends or family, finding common interests is key to forming and maintaining bonds. Secretive Scorpions could adore a good mystery, so a day out solving an escape room or a night in discussing this month's thriller book club choice could be two great ways for a Scorpio to bond with their suspense-seeking friends; Virgo's methodical analysis could make them the perfect partner for helping Scorpios get to the bottom of a crime or an extrovert Leo friend will no doubt jump at the chance to arrange a murder mystery in a spooky house for all of their friendship group to enjoy.

Another passion of sumptuous Scorpio is food and drink, whether it be opening an expensive bottle of wine at home or enjoying the tasting menu at the latest Michelin star restaurant in town. Scorpio's negative energy could have them spending all day at home, whipping up a gluttonous feast for their family and friends to enjoy, whom likely will be quite familiar with Scorpio's culinary talents. Venus-ruled signs Libra and Taurus are friends that will happily indulge in Scorpio's love for luxury and will probably be the ones bringing over the bottles of champagne to their Scorpio host.

Scorpios can be emotionally intuitive parents; if there is something amiss with Scorpio's child, or any family member, this sign could readily pick up on it and be set on fixing whatever the problem is for their loved one. The Scorpion's love for their family is intense and their protective nature is formidable to challenge, so loved ones should rest assured that Scorpio has their back through thick and thin. The possessive and jealous side of a Scorpio could rear its unsightly head when it comes to those that this sign treasures most. Scorpio will indeed love their family like treasure and they will no doubt be the most valuable thing in this sign's life, but they should avoid treating people like possessions and trust their family to always return to them. Empowering their friends and family rather than using their own power over them will be key in maintaining happy and successful relationships for Scorpio.

MONEY AND CAREERS

....

Being a certain star sign will not dictate the type of career that you have, although the characteristics that fall under each sign could help you identify the areas in which you could potentially thrive. Conversely, to succeed in the workplace, it is just as important to understand what you are good at as it is to know what you are less brilliant at so that you can see the areas in which you will need to perhaps work harder to achieve your career and financial goals.

Committed Scorpios aren't inclined to flit between jobs, unless they are still figuring out what they want to set their mind to. Scorpio's immense dedication may well see them stay in the same job or working for the same company for many years, whether they are 100% happy in it or not. A Scorpio devoted to their career should make sure that it comes from a place of passion rather than complacency. Scorpios can value security above their job satisfaction, and if they fear failure then they may decide to not try anything too daring. Channelling the influence of Mars, Scorpio should dare to dream and actively chase after their career goals with courage.

Scorpio's single-minded approach to life can mean that they lose themselves obsessively in their work, so it helps if they are passionate about their career. A sign as mysterious as Scorpio will often be attracted to the obscure or shadowy and won't shy away from darker occupations. Whether it's making an indie horror film inspired by fellow Scorpio Martin Scorsese, writing a thriller novel, or working in a funeral home, what might give other people nightmares could be the Scorpion's career calling.

Scorpios tend to be very private, especially when it comes to their bank accounts; asking a Scorpio about their salary could feel like asking them to strip down to their underwear. However, it might be clear from Scorpio's lavish spending habits as to how well they are doing financially. High earning jobs certainly will suit the shopaholic Scorpio who enjoys treating themselves to the very best of everything. Remember, this sign is about quality over quantity so whilst their shopping bags may be few, what lays inside them is likely to be of high value. The secrecy around spending and their funds may mean that they choose to keep some of their finances under wraps, even from their spouses.

Whilst you can't always choose who you work with, it can be advantageous to learn about colleagues' key characteristics through their star signs to try and work out the best ways of working with them. Hardworking Capricorns can bring structure and order to the work life of a Scorpio and make sure their passion for a project does not fizzle out before it has reached fruition. Signs with a strong influence of Mercury, like Virgo and Gemini will offer their thoughts and opinions willingly to a Scorpio seeking advice and can be important colleagues to bounce ideas off.

HEALTH AND WELLBEING

· · · · · · · · · · · · · · · · · ·

The scorpion is known for being able to withstand almost anything, freeze this creature solid and then thaw it out and this durable wonder can still be alive! Similarly, Scorpios (minus the freezing bit) can endure serious hardship and deep emotional grievances. These folks are certainly made of hardy stock, but their water element can make them feel pain deeper than most and make their inner power hard to channel at times. Scorpios are undoubtedly strong, but their tendency to isolate themselves in times of stress can sometimes weaken them as they close themselves off to any outside support. This controlling sign may struggle to ask for help and allow their vulnerability to be exposed but asking for help is never a sign of weakness and should only help strengthen Scorpio.

When a stressed-out Scorpion is feeling overwhelmed, they can turn to escapism for an immediate solution to their problems; binging on box sets, wrapped up in a blanket, and still wearing their pyjamas may be a familiar scenario. Whilst cocooning themselves away like this, with a trashy movie, may feel initially comforting they should be careful of doing this too regularly as it could also start to have the reverse effect. Losing themselves in a good book or spending time with an Aries or Leo friend who they have not seen in a while and will be happy to talk about themselves for an hour or two could be a far more positive distraction. Hearing about the problems of others may give some healing perspective to Scorpio's own issues, or at the very least will strengthen their friendship ties and make both parties feel happier from having taken the time to catch up.

Whilst this sensitive sign may be the best of all the water signs at controlling their emotions thanks to the influence of Pluto, Scorpio's sting of aggression will usually pierce their victim with the strongest of venom. Fortunately for everyone, this Scorpion's scorn is usually infrequent, but trying to avoid big bursts of aggression is still an important lesson for this sign to learn. Scorpios can have a wonderful sense of humour, so trying to channel a lighter mood that allows them to laugh at life rather than going on the attack will hopefully diffuse any internal aggression from building up. Scorpions are intense by nature and their serious side is dominant, but inviting fun into their lives and not taking things too seriously should help to balance out their moods.

With the influence of Mars and Pluto, Scorpio can have a lot of powerful energy that if left unreleased can cause emotional and physical discomfort. Teamwork isn't always a Scorpio's forte, their negative energy and fixed mode lends itself well to working alone, however, a little healthy competition can really fuel Scorpio's energy; signing up to a running or swimming race could rid Scorpio of their restless energy and set positive goals for them. If it's a surplus of emotional energy that is building up in this water sign, then finding ways to sensitively release what is inside of them is also imperative; writing poems or a novel could be a positive outlet for this emotional sign as well as always seeking out professional therapy if necessary.

Scorpio

. . . .

DAILY FORECASTS
for 2020

OCTOBER
· · · · · · · · · · · · · · · · ·

Thursday 1st

October begins with a Full Moon in your health and duties sector. With Mars currently retrograding there, you should now be able to see clearly how your time is separated. This opportunity is also great for making mini resolutions to spend more time on yourself and your personal goals.

Friday 2nd

Venus is moving into your social sector today. This is good news in the run-up to the festive season. There will be more harmony now between friendship factions. She is also insisting that you balance time for friends and time for you. Expect a lot of dining out whilst she is here.

Saturday 3rd

The Moon and Taurus are making a lovely earthy connection today, which will help you to feel grounded. This may feel alien to you, but stick with it. You may find a new love within your social groups. This influence will also show how you split time between lovers and friends.

Sunday 4th

Today, you may find that your heart and your head are not in synchronisation. Mercury is in Scorpio and wants to think and talk deeply, whilst your emotional body just wants to be cared for by sensual things like love, food and money. This may cause some unrest within you.

Monday 5th

Pluto, your secondary ruler, turns direct today. This is like a deep breath out, and you should feel the tension leaving your body. This means that all the planets in your communications sector are up and running. Education, trips and new learning experiences are getting the green light now.

Tuesday 6th

The Moon enters your sector of sex, death and rebirth. Endings and beginnings are foremost in your mind. You have the ability to transform something rather than throw it out completely. This can be a skill of yours, if you do not let emotions guide your thinking.

Wednesday 7th

You will need to watch your words today. This will involve important relationships and lovers. Mercury in your own sector of self sits opposite the planet of disruption. Alternatively, this influence may make you come up with something ingenious.

Thursday 8th

You will be thinking again about travel and settling elsewhere in the world. This is just a whim at the moment, but may turn into something more concrete when Mars turns direct again. Your roots are important, but you have a yearning to set down new ones in foreign lands.

Friday 9th

Mars and Pluto, your planetary rulers, are locked in a dispute today. Mars, who represents your energy and drive, will lose. This may manifest as a control issue, which will leave you exhausted. This is a sign to look after yourself more and to get your energy levels back up to normal.

Saturday 10th

There may be a lovely surprise for you today, as Venus is sweet-talking Uranus in your relationship sector. He is in a sign that she rules, which means that he'll listen. Expect to be spoiled or do the spoiling today. It's the weekend, so what are you waiting for?

Sunday 11th

There's no need to be a Sunday worker today. If there's something that needs to be done for your boss, do it at your own pace, as your lover or an important person wants to spend the rest of the weekend with you. Put the work down and get back to playing.

Monday 12th

You will be able to concentrate on your work today, as the Moon is entering your career sector. As you may already have had work on your mind yesterday, you're motivated and know what needs to be done. Colleagues will look to you for advice and feed on your motivation. You are in good spirits.

Tuesday 13th

The Sun is shining directly on Mars in your health and duties sector today. Take this as a neon light that you are doing too much. This may be the reason your health has been suffering lately. Let something go in order to lighten your load. Even Mars cannot move forwards again with too much on his shoulders.

Wednesday 14th

Just when you might have thought it was all plain sailing, Mercury goes retrograde in Scorpio. In your area of self, this will be about your own psyche. He will go back into deep, dark corners and reassess things he thought he had dealt with.

Thursday 15th

The energy today suggests that you may have trouble with someone trying to undermine you or steal your glory. This is also about reviewing your communication and education, and asking yourself if this is really what you want. Can you do this? Stop doubting yourself.

Friday 16th

A New Moon in your dreams sector highlights that Scorpian need for intensity and mystery. You may now make intentions and affirmations to work more on your inner self. You are no stranger to psychology and spirituality, and have a knack for combining these two together. You will do well at this.

Saturday 17th

This could be an intense day where emotions simmer like a volcano ready to erupt. You may have an irresistible urge to say what's on your mind and in your heart. This will almost certainly result in a lava flow or an earthquake, and you must be prepared for the consequences.

Sunday 18th

You may feel quite rebellious today. You have great teachers in front of you, but you have found your own voice and done your own research. You may be pushing boundaries with elders. This is all part of the learning experience and a good teacher will recognise this.

Monday 19th

You may feel extremely tired today. Mars and Venus are in connection with Jupiter, who makes everything bigger. Mars is exhausted and Venus is putting more and more tasks his way, via Jupiter. Have a day indoors and in your own familiar environment. Eat and sleep well.

Tuesday 20th

Do you remember that Mercury is currently retrograde? This is an unstable time for everyone, and he may be rocking the boat in your relationships now. Mercurian issues are usually about misunderstood or cruel conversations. Watch out for this, and do not be the one speaking words that hurt.

Wednesday 21st

The Moon is settling into your communications sector today, so your learning activities will take up some of your time. This is something that you are really putting your heart into and is fast becoming a labour of love. Venus is busy transforming social acquaintances into educational allies. You will soon have a support team.

Thursday 22nd

The Sun is moving into Scorpio today, making this your birthday month. You may feel tired and not really in the mood to do your educational activities, nor your regular duties. Do what you can but reserve some energy for what excites you.

Friday 23rd

Families are featured today and may give you a break from routine. A friendly family get-together sounds like a good idea, but Mercury retrograde may want to say the wrong thing and risk upsetting someone. Keep it light and carefree. There's no need to rake up the past.

Saturday 24th

New friends and allies on your learning journey will become important now. These could be people from groups on social media or people you have met physically. All are valuable and can point you in the right direction with your new interests. Learn from each other.

Sunday 25th

Mercury is lost in the glare of the Sun and is saying nothing for once. Use this time to think and not speak. This is a receptive, passive time rather than one to share what you know. Process the new information you have received recently before overloading yourself. Make sure there is room in your head for it all.

Monday 26th

A poetic Moon is making sweet connections to the Sun and Mercury, who are both in Scorpio. It also has a stabilising effect on anything that could disturb the status quo. Make the most of this energy. Although you thrive off drama, this peace will fill your soul.

Tuesday 27th

Dreams and visions could get a boost now. Using symbols and metaphors will come easily, and you will be able to put these to good use. Explorations of the psyche, your education and creative projects all benefit from this influence. You are quite the poet at the moment.

Wednesday 28th

Today, your dream sector is bookended by Venus, entering at the beginning, and Mercury, flying into it backwards. Love, peace and harmony are added to your solitude and peaceful moments. Enquiry and conversation enhance your shared time. Connection to a divine source is possible now.

Thursday 29th

The Moon is meeting up with a weary Mars in your health and duties sector today, which could leave you feeling emotionally drained. There may also be a feeling of guilt about duties you have neglected recently. Don't feel guilty. This area is draining, and you have done the best you can.

Friday 30th

Your relationships and the important people in your life need attention now. This will be beneficial if you have a mutually receptive partner. Otherwise, this will add to the energy loss and may make you feel worse. Put your other interests to one side.

Saturday 31st

A Full Moon occurs today in your relationship sector. This is the second Full Moon in a calendar month and is known as a Blue Moon. It will highlight the imbalance in love relationships. You will be more moody than usual. Make sure that your needs are met.

NOVEMBER

· · · · · · · · · · · · · · · · · · ·

Sunday 1st

The veil falls and you can see a situation for what it really is now. All the mist and illusion will be burnt away and you will be left staring at the real thing. This will come as a big shock. The question is, what are you going to do about it? The choice is yours.

Monday 2nd

Your attention will shift today, and you will now be probing the whys and wherefores of recent events. You've possibly had a shock to your system and will not let things go. You begin a psychological analysis of the circumstances that lead you to be involved with a certain person.

Tuesday 3rd

Emotionally, you will be balanced today. Venus is busy bringing you peace in your alone time and Mars is quiet for once. Attending to the daily grind will give you some stability. You may be called upon to mediate a situation. If this is your situation, make no judgements until all sides are presented.

Wednesday 4th

Mercury is turning direct in your dreams sector today, so you may need some time to yourself for the next few days. Reflect on what has transpired during his retrograde period. This part of your chart rules endings. You may bring something to a close now and you can do it with love.

Thursday 5th

You may be thinking seriously about travelling or settling elsewhere at the moment. Be mindful that this influence isn't owing to recent events but is a passing Moon phase in your travel sector. Don't make any rash moves right now. Venus is butting in and also discouraging you.

Friday 6th

You may feel despondent about your education and learning activities today. Resentment is hanging over you like a cloud, and you may feel as if you are stuck. Lie low and take the time to pause and reflect. Don't beat yourself up about this situation.

Saturday 7th

You need a distraction today and may have brought work home for the weekend. Your natural instinct is to make good use of time. Quietly working away at unfinished projects or those you have neglected will bring a greater peace. Prepare to rise above it all like the other Scorpio symbol, the eagle.

Sunday 8th

This could be a tough Sunday for you. There's a lot going through your mind, but the energy of the Sun and Moon will not allow for progress. This is like a stalemate move in chess. What happens now? Nothing. The game has to end.

Monday 9th

Recent tensions will return today as Venus and Mars move opposite each other. This elaborates on the stalemate situation of yesterday. It's a 'me and you' or 'us and them' stand-off. Men and women will be in power struggles now. This is also about how you present yourself and how you hide.

Tuesday 10th

Mercury is on that critical last degree of your entire chart. This is about a closure where there can be no going back. You must process what's in your head now, once and for all. Mercury will leave the very deepest point of your chart with clear instructions on how to proceed.

Wednesday 11th

You might receive some revelations about how the educational activities that have interested you all year could be your way forwards. You have been looking for a vocation that's inspirational. You can make this into your soul's purpose and become a leader. This is worth the hard work.

Thursday 12th

Today will bring refreshment and new insight. The Moon and Venus are meeting in your dream sector and will uplift you. Mercury is ready for his new mission in your sector of self. Jupiter and Pluto are making huge changes in your communications sector. You will see many positive transformations. Things are looking up.

Friday 13th

The Moon is entering Scorpio, which is when your best work can be done and you can connect deeply to almost anything you are passionate about. The Moon will meet Mercury, and your heart and mind will be in synchronisation. This is the best news.

Saturday 14th

You can breathe deeply again. Mars has turned direct, so forward movement, assertiveness and motivation will return. This is a great time to begin a new fitness regime. In fact, this is a great time to begin anything at all and the chances are that you will stick at it.

Sunday 15th

A New Moon in Scorpio offers the chance to recommit to working on your inner self. The only person who can reach your depths is you. The skill set to do this is part of what makes up the Scorpian personality. Make intentions and affirmations now.

Monday 16th

There may be some conflict within you today. This is likely to be about you doubting your own abilities to be successful with the goals you have been setting for yourself. Trust that this is what is meant for you, and that the right path has finally shown itself. Venus is in her element in your dreams sector. Love, money and stability are possibilities now.

Tuesday 17th

There are times when you look back at how far you have come. This could be one of them. If you're doing the necessary self-development, then skills learnt in the past can be used again now. You may get some genius ideas today.

Wednesday 18th

Do you feel that you have taken on too much? This is quite
normal for you, but know that you can do it. Hesitation may
creep in, so you will need more motivation. This is going to
be a big step into the unknown, but you are no stranger to
exploring foreign territory.

Thursday 19th

You should be able to conquer yesterday's self-doubt today,
allowing your heart to fill with passion again. Wise teachers
are making themselves known to you now. Learn what you
can from others who have walked this path before you. Find a
way to make this journey unique and own it. Step outside your
comfort zone.

Friday 20th

As the Moon enters your family sector, you may face resistance
from family members. There may be a lot of discussion concerning
your individuality within the group. Maternal figures will show
concern and may attempt to veer you away from the path that
you're on. This is their way of showing their love for you.

Saturday 21st

The Sun will leave Scorpio while Venus will enter it. Your money
sector will get an energetic boost and light will shine on any areas
that need attention. Venus will restore your sense of self-worth
and bring you more peace. Your new journey will be set now.

Sunday 22nd

You may want to finish up old projects. Romance is in the air, but that air needs clearing first. You could be in love with creative pursuits. A new quest is beckoning, and you will be compelled to follow. This is typical of you, ever the seeker and the eternal student.

Monday 23rd

The Moon is making some delightful contacts, which will make you feel as light as a feather. Everything looks positive, and you may ask yourself if this is too good to be true. Just enjoy the feeling and stop sabotaging yourself. Good things are coming your way.

Tuesday 24th

Mercury is whispering across to Neptune. He's telling the planet of dreams what the new plans are. Make sure that you have no illusions about your new journey. Mercury can be somewhat of a magician in Scorpio, but you can use this energy to manifest your desires and ground them in reality.

Wednesday 25th

Before all great heroes begin their quest, they need to check that they are strong enough. Now would be a good time to visit the health centre and get general check-ups done. You may need extra vitamins or support to be on top form.

Thursday 26th

You will have a day where you just cannot gather the energy you need. However, don't be disheartened by this. The Moon is sitting on top of Mars, and he is unable to move. The weight of your emotions can sometimes overcome your energy and drive. Stick with it; this will soon pass.

Friday 27th

If somebody told you not to do something, then what would you do? Of course, you will do the opposite, won't you! You may be digging your heels in or having a little temper tantrum. This is a day for you, so don't let anyone else dictate your actions.

Saturday 28th

You may fall back into a dream world and create a fantasy land in your head. Your mind may wander, but this is fine. Be mindful that there's a real world and an imaginary world. Try not to be too unrealistic now, as you will only be disappointed later on.

Sunday 29th

Today, you can show people what you are made of. You will want to talk to others about your new plans, but be careful that you do not go over the top and brag. Try not to come across as egotistical. You could be overly talkative.

Monday 30th

A Full Moon occurs in your sex, death and rebirth sector today. What is being illuminated now? What has come to completion from six months ago? A partial eclipse throws a shadow over the Moon, suggesting there is something lurking in a corner that you may have forgotten about.

DECEMBER

······················

Tuesday 1st

Mercury is entering your money sector now. With a bit of
luck, his role as the planet of merchants will help with a bit
of buying and selling. You may want to buy items for your
home environment that have a touch of the exotic about
them. This could be fun.

Wednesday 2nd

As the Moon drifts into your travel sector, you may realise
a few things. Your interest and educational pursuits are an
exploration that is personal to you. Mercury adds his influence
and lets you see how far you travel in your mind. Make your
home and learning your new travel adventures.

Thursday 3rd

You may feel duty-bound today. There's no time for dreaming
now and you must simply get on with things. You could be
feeling a little unwell, but don't worry; this is a payback for all
the adrenaline you have been using lately. Home comforts will
help you feel better.

Friday 4th

Have you thought about asking for a raise at work? Mercury is
making a great connection to the Moon in your career sector
today and he will lend you the gift of the gab. Don't forget that
he's also in your money sector, so this is worth a try.

Saturday 5th

The recent energy will lift today, helping you to march along with your head held high. There may be some disruption in your important relationships that may affect your working day. The important other may be someone in work, so be warned that this unrest could come from both areas.

Sunday 6th

Venus will find a way of giving your self-worth a boost, reminding you that you don't have to make sacrifices to get ahead. She's allowing you to dream big and go after what you desire. Her connection to Neptune is emphasising this. Love may be on its way.

Monday 7th

Your social sector will get some attention today. There could be some nice surprises within your friendship groups. How about starting the festive season with a get-together with someone you haven't seen for a while? Social media groups could also bring some fun revelations and unconventional thinking.

Tuesday 8th

Saturn is at the critical degree of your communications sector today. He will be here for ten days, so it's time to learn a very important lesson. This is likely to be about personal boundaries and how much you take on. Think hard about this issue now.

Wednesday 9th

The Sun in your money sector is burning away any illusions that you may have had regarding finances. Perhaps you have been overspending and thought this was okay? This is a time when the bank balance needs to be checked before splurging on unnecessary items of luxury.

Thursday 10th

Venus is in Scorpio today, where she is sweet-talking Pluto. The result is that females will be able to get what they want and will be able to control situations normally dominated by the men in their lives. There will be a light-hearted feel in the air, and much laughter.

Friday 11th

Today, there's a lot of movement and activity. The Sun in your money sector is connecting to Mars in your duties sector. This is looking like an expensive season for you. There may be a battle between you and an important person, possibly a partner. You're not on the same wavelength today.

Saturday 12th

The Moon and Venus join up today, and the energy is overtly feminine. Venus is the witch or the sorceress in Scorpio and here comes the priestess Moon. Today can be a very sensual day. Be sure to make the most of it.

Sunday 13th

As the Moon moves into your money sector, you may feel a little guilty about your spending habits lately. However, this doesn't stop you wanting to make your home into an exotic paradise or a Renaissance art gallery. You may bring your foreign pleasures to your own space and create a new comfort zone.

Monday 14th

There is a New Moon in your money and possessions sector today. Mercury is also at the same spot, and he is giving you ideas to use as affirmations and intentions regarding this sector. Is he urging you to spend or save? Does he want you to buy or sell? Listen carefully for clues around you.

Tuesday 15th

Venus is leaving your area of self and wandering into your money house. As she rules money, this could be a time of gain or even more spending on luxuries. There is work to be done in your health and duties sector, and Mars gets on with the daily routine to avoid spending.

Wednesday 16th

You have a vision of where you would like your new work to go. Self-control is the attitude you must approach to ground this in reality. This is your project and therefore no one can understand it the way you do. You're on top of it now.

Thursday 17th

This is an important day, as the Moon is making great connections with those planets that have been dominating your communications sector. Firstly, Jupiter fires up your passion and brings you luck. Then, the Moon drifts into your family sector and meets Saturn, who blesses you with self-discipline.

Friday 18th

Mercury is in the heart of the Sun in your money house. You must sit quietly and listen to the information he is receiving now. This will be important for your finances and your home environment. Is there anything more that you need to collect or research in this area?

Saturday 19th

Jupiter is spending his last day in your communications sector. Think of this like Santa Clause coming early and hiding a gift somewhere. The bringer of joy and luck is bestowing you with good karma before he moves on to another area of your chart. You will find that gift now.

Sunday 20th

This is another important day, as Jupiter meets up with Saturn. This is happening right at the beginning of your family sector. Fathers and sons will feature greatly. Other paternal figures or heads of authority may have a confrontation or a blessed reunion. Feel the love here.

Monday 21st

The Winter Solstice arrives now. Both the Sun and Mercury
enter your communications sector and pause for reflection
before the wheel of the year turns and the days start getting
longer. This is a time of rest before the busy festive season.
Look back at the year you have had and give thanks.

Tuesday 22nd

You will have already felt the rush of excitement as the
Moon passes into your health and duties sector, but you
must now make sure that all jobs are completed before the
Christmas break. Make sure that your health is good, as this
season may drain your resources.

Wednesday 23rd

There may be a battle of wills today or simply a rush to get things
prepared for the festivities. Somebody wants to take control of the
whole proceedings and will not accept help. If you must opt out
and let others get on with it, do so.

Thursday 24th

Spend some time with your lover or another special person today.
The Moon is in Taurus and you could find this energy tense.
If you're alone, be good to yourself. You don't have to see
anyone if you would rather spend time on your own.

Friday 25th

As the Moon meets up with Uranus, the planet of disruption,
hopefully the surprises will be good ones. Mercury wants to
have his say in your communications sector and, true to form,
he has you making a lot of short trips. This could be a busy
Christmas Day for you.

Saturday 26th

The calm after the storm brings a much warmer and quieter energy. The busy day has been and gone, and you can now just sit quietly and feel in total control. Sharing this time with someone special will bring even greater satisfaction.

Sunday 27th

You will have time to reflect now. However, this will not be on a superficial level, knowing you. You want to analyse the year behind you and eke out the reasoning behind the more difficult moments. Learn to let it go. That door has closed. Stop thinking of the ifs and buts and get ready to move forwards without looking backwards.

Monday 28th

You will be better able to shift your focus now to the year ahead, today. There will be much teaching, learning and sharing of information. Your intellectual pursuits will bring you an acclaim you never thought you would have. You have surprised yourself, but now prepare to surpass yourself. Give yourself some credit.

Tuesday 29th

There's a Full Moon in your travel sector. At one time, getting away was all you could think about. You now realise that reading books, watching documentaries or researching other cultures can bring you all the travel adventures you require. Your inquisitive mind is your travel guide.

Wednesday 30th

Mercury is in opposition to the Moon, today, and is reminding you that you actually do have the ability to make a career around your persistent studies. Venus has you spending too much again. You may even be falling in love now. Just stay grounded and remember that you have great work to do.

Thursday 31st

Venus is joining a point where you can look back at the past today. Long-lost loves may come back into your mind yet disappear again quickly. You are feeling whimsical and ready to see the year out with love, peace and harmony. Happy New Year!

Scorpio

DAILY FORECASTS
for 2021

JANUARY

· · · · · · · · · · · · · · · · ·

Friday 1st

Happy New Year and welcome to 2021. You begin the year on the back of a Full Moon in your travel sector. Home life and exploration can be a constant conundrum for you. Safety and security come first in order for you to explore to your heart's delight. The Moon in your career sector helps you to glow today.

Saturday 2nd

Your leadership qualities are noticed at this time of the month; you may not realise just how much people look up to you. Mars is in the last few degrees of your health and duties sector. Now is the time to make resolutions regarding mundane jobs and fitness.

Sunday 3rd

The Moon shifts into your social sector, giving you extra energy to enjoy with friends. Brainstorming with your social groups can produce great plans for the year ahead. Bright ideas and enthusiastic people combine to start the year off with an exciting, rebellious and worthy list of social activities.

Monday 4th

Neptune is trying to beguile you with flights of fancy. Romantic notions and artistic pursuits fill your head today. It's difficult to concentrate on anything else. Get out your planner and fill in some possible dates for engagements with friends. You may also think about decluttering your friendships now.

Tuesday 5th

The trickster Mercury meets Pluto today in your communications sector. Listen out for hidden messages and be ready to read between the lines of everything. Pluto is one of your rulers and he asks that you transform or end something. Mercury is finding out what this is. Keep your ears open today.

Wednesday 6th

Mars spends his final day in your health and duties sector. You may find that you have extra jobs to do. Maybe these have been outstanding for some time. Use your ruler's energy to get things up to speed. He also encourages you to check in with your health right now.

Thursday 7th

Mars moves into your relationship sector. Expect things to get a little hotter now. Mars rules your sex drive as well as your stamina. Be warned, he is temperamental and hot-headed; you can be too assertive in your close relationships and this might not go down too well.

Friday 8th

Today you may get an idea of what Pluto is asking you to change. Mercury contacts the Moon and you get an emotional trigger. The Moon reaches your own sign and you become secretive or super-sensitive. Don't let your intense emotions get the better of you. Let the triggers teach you something.

Saturday 9th

Mercury enters your family sector today. Interactions with your nearest and dearest will be off the scale now. Gossip, arguments or camaraderie are all features of Mercury's influence. This can be an unusual time of high activity. A connection to Mars can make things volatile. Be careful.

Sunday 10th

Mercury now bumps into stern Saturn. It's likely that you come under scrutiny and clash with a family elder. As the Moon moves into your finance and value sector, you should take a good look at your bank balance. There is something exotic you wish to buy for your home.

Monday 11th

Jupiter now has the pleasure of meeting speedy Mercury. The big, jolly, luck-bringing planet has words with inquisitive Mercury. Someone in your family will enjoy your company today. An older authority figure can provide you with intellectual stimulation. Take on board any wise words you receive from them today.

Tuesday 12th

Be careful today. Mercury and Uranus are squaring off. You must watch what you say, as you may be prone to spread gossip or let out a secret. This will involve your family and close partnerships. The Moon in your communications sector asks that you be responsible and adult about it.

Wednesday 13th

A New Moon in your communications sector allows you to set goals and intentions regarding your intellectual pursuits. Perhaps you have been wanting to make a trip or a short course of study. Plan now. There will be a lot of tension in close relationships today, so tread carefully.

Thursday 14th

The Sun meets Pluto. This energy is asking you to burn away and compost excess baggage. You have the power to transform lead into gold now, if you wish. Moon contacts today will make you unstable and prone to listen to your self-talk. Cut through the rubbish and hidden treasure.

Friday 15th

Today, the best thing you can do is to spend time with family. The Moon has passed the planets residing in the early degrees and now lets you relax. Take time to appreciate how wonderful and wacky your family is. Celebrate how individual you all are. Enjoy the diversity.

Saturday 16th

This is an ideal day for any romantic ventures. Writing, art, and music are all favoured by the Moon in your creative sector, today. Make the most of this beautiful energy and woo the one you love with a poem or song. You're idealistic and wish to merge with another.

Sunday 17th

The Moon meets Neptune today. Your emotions can be lost at sea. If surrender is how you prefer to experience connection, then go for it. Just be sure not to sacrifice yourself and become a martyr. Keep one foot on the shore while the other is in Neptune's depths.

Monday 18th

You're likely to be in a fighting mood. The Moon in your health and duties sector gives you the emotional energy you need to start a fresh week. You're highly motivated and eager to crack on with your chores. Be mindful not to tread on anyone's toes.

Tuesday 19th

The Sun shifts signs and lands in your family sector. This may well feel like a spotlight is illuminating your tribe. You might feel the warmth of it or feel too exposed and embarrassed. Venus is attempting to bring love and harmony to your communication style, but today you may speak out of turn.

Wednesday 20th

The two disruptive planets meet today. Mars, your ruler, bumps into Uranus, so all hell could break loose in your relationships. This highly charged energy can be volatile or super-sexy. It will be unexpected and there will be nothing you can do to prevent it. Use it wisely.

Thursday 21st

The Moon moves into your relationship sector. You may be able to soften the blow of any conflict. However, difficult connections to Saturn and Jupiter will make you feel like a naughty child. Get out of the way of the fall-out. Take cover or get hurt.

Friday 22nd

Good connections to Venus and Pluto today mean that any recent crisis can now be smoothed over. The debris can become ground for new growth, something beautiful even. You may have fallen head over heels in love and not realised it. Your head and heart need to have a deep conversation.

Saturday 23rd

A lovely contact between Venus and Neptune brings you back to your creative projects or love pursuits. The Moon shifts into your intimacy sector where you are questioning everything. Over-analysis is not good for you, especially if it concerns a love interest. Put those thoughts to paper, instead.

Sunday 24th

The Sun meets Saturn. This could manifest as a clash of egos or a parent/child incident. Saturn is the harsh teacher and the Sun represents ego and essence. Someone may try to dumb you down and prevent you from shining. This could be a useful lesson. It might also be manipulation. Scrutinise the details of the bigger picture before reacting.

Monday 25th

Mars and Jupiter are squaring off today. Mars is in your relationship sector, whilst Jupiter is spreading the joy in your family sector. There may be a conflict of interests for you in these areas. Mars always wants to get ahead, whereas Jupiter may be the heavy weight dragging you back.

Tuesday 26th

Emotionally, you feel safer in your own environment today.
You can travel far in your mind or by watching documentaries
but, for you, your home is your world. If you're feeling a little
tense, treat yourself to a foreign take-away or watch a cultural
film tonight.

Wednesday 27th

You might still feel as if you are far away from home today.
Neptune is calling and you may drift off to fantasy or foreign
lands in your mind. Pluto and Venus are asking you to think
about a course of study, maybe learning a language.

Thursday 28th

A bright Full Moon in your career sector shows how you lead.
You have the essence of a courageous spirit in your chosen
career. You can be bold and brave here. You may feel restricted
and experience inequality, but you should know that you are
admired for your strength and compassion in the workplace.

Friday 29th

Today has beautiful energy for you to access. The Moon in your
fiery career sector asks you to be brave. The Sun meets Jupiter
in your family sector and blesses your tribe with fortune and
abundance. How will you celebrate this? A family meal or
activity could be fun.

Saturday 30th

Today you should back up all of your devices and double check
all travel plans. Mercury goes retrograde tomorrow, so use
today to prepare. A social evening with friendship groups can
round the day off nicely. Serve your friends and notice the
balance of give and take here.

Sunday 31st

Mercury turns retrograde in your family sector. You must be careful not to upset elders or authority figures now. Misunderstandings can be taken too far. Conflict between family members can be smoothed over if you practise pausing before responding. Learn to stop reacting and consider your next move before responding.

FEBRUARY

····················

Monday 1st

Venus moves into your family sector today. This will be a great
help to you when trying to navigate Mercury retrograde; she
will bring balance and harmony while here. Mars and the Sun
are at odds today. You will see conflict between family and close
relationships. Use the energy that Venus brings.

Tuesday 2nd

The Moon is in your hidden sector. You are already a secretive
sign who over-analyses and seeks justification for everything.
However, the Moon makes some nice connections here and
enables you to be positive today. Your private thoughts surprise
and make you smile inwardly.

Wednesday 3rd

This afternoon, the Moon enters your sign. Your natural intensity
amps up and people will see you as overtly Scorpian. Mercury and
Pluto help you to make an emotional judgement call. You're able
to bring an end to something or complete a long-standing project.
There may be quarrels with lovers, today, or a lack of compromise.

Thursday 4th

Today, the Moon will sit opposite the two volatile planets in
your relationship sector. This suggests a difficult day for you.
You may find that your shadow side comes out or projection
is going on in your close relationships. You are stubborn and
unwilling to comply right now.

Friday 5th

It's likely that Mercury retrograde gets you into trouble.
The Moon in your sign is badly connecting to Mercury. Your
jealous stinger may surface. Be mindful of how you speak to
family members. Be clear and direct. Your words must match
your feelings, or you must say nothing at all.

Saturday 6th

There's much better energy available to you today. Venus
and Saturn meet up and, although Saturn can be harsh,
Venus can win him over. You are being tested on your
respect for authority figures. The Moon in your sector of
finance and value lets you know your worth.

Sunday 7th

The Moon crosses the point of past karma in your finances
sector. You may now have to deal with old issues regarding
money, possessions and self-worth. Remembering skills and
lessons from the past will help you progress now. You could
experience an unexpected hiccup with a lover today.

Monday 8th

Mercury has nothing to say. Your job is to listen for hidden
messages, dream symbols and any communication that comes
to you. You may be itching to get something started with a
lover or business partner, but you should wait until Mercury
retrograde is over. Keep your ears open.

Tuesday 9th

The Moon makes good connections to both of your rulers.
You might have picked up on Mercury's messages to you and
may now know what to do with them. Mars makes you driven
and eager to please; Pluto helps you take control and make it
happen. This is something new.

Wednesday 10th

The Moon enters your family sector. There's such a lot going on
here right now. You feel like rebelling and hugging everyone at
the same time. The energy is up and down. The best thing you
can do is to go with the flow and learn to be more adaptable for
this period.

Thursday 11th

Today there's a New Moon in your busy family sector. Set goals
and intentions to expand and enhance your family interactions.
The Moon meets Mercury; you should be careful with words.
Venus and Jupiter also have a date and bless your family sector.

Friday 12th

As the Moon shifts into your creative sector, you might find
that your day seems almost dream-like. You set yourself
up for a romantic weekend. Surprises may come from your
relationship sector. Perhaps your love interest has the same
ideas as you. Spend time connecting on a new level with
someone special.

Saturday 13th

Words of love will need to be very clear and not ambiguous today. Neptune is highly featured, and he can throw a mist over things and make them seem unreal. There's a chance you see only what you want to now. Mercury and Venus meet up to help your loving intentions be completely understood.

Sunday 14th

Enjoy the rest of the weekend in your love bubble. When it bursts this evening, you'll be ready for focused activity. Mercury meets Jupiter; be warned that this can mean retrograde effects get larger or out of control. Jupiter brings luck but also the expansion of everything he touches.

Monday 15th

Today, it's possible to get everyone in the family on board and come to an agreement of some sort. The Moon is well placed in your duties sector to ensure that all those planets in there behave nicely. You can lead meetings and negotiate your own terms with ease.

Tuesday 16th

Your desire to forge ahead with plans may be disrupted by someone wishing to take control. Your powers of persuasion will come in handy now. Venus helps you to do this with grace and beauty. This is only a slight interruption; you can resume action soon enough.

Wednesday 17th

As the Moon enters your relationship sector, it meets Uranus the unpredictable planet. You will find that you cannot please everyone all of the time. Will you mediate, or choose between family and lovers today? It's up to you to make a responsible and adult decision. Expect the unexpected right now.

Thursday 18th

The Sun enters your creative sector. This is a great time for love and romance, connecting with spiritual people or making art and music. You may just find your muse now. Be careful not to argue with lovers or important partners when the Moon meets assertive Mars.

Friday 19th

The celestial lovers, Venus and Mars, are at odds. This will influence your family and relationships sector. Mars is your ruler, so you will be more inclined to be direct than to achieve harmony. You can be in control of an awkward situation but don't become a bully.

Saturday 20th

Your mind will be full of ideas and concepts that are deep and mysterious today. This is nothing new to you. Moon connections suggest that you take time to look into finances you share with another, as they may no longer suit your needs. Jupiter expands your mind with a search for truth.

Sunday 21st

Mercury turns direct. You can now sign contracts or make travel plans without unnecessary worry. Venus enters your mind space with thoughts of desire. Perhaps you're thinking of getting to know someone on a deeper level. You're most certainly thinking about the future, now.

Monday 22nd

The Moon reaches your travel sector and has you evaluating plans to seek beyond your comfort zone. A pleasant connection to the Sun in your creative sector helps you to make steps towards a person you have been shy about. Do it, you may surprise yourself by acting impulsively.

Tuesday 23rd

Watery energy makes you more sensitive than usual. You may be emotionally unstable today or you may just be drifting off to see what lies beneath the depths. Superficiality doesn't suffice today. You wish to be nurtured by exploring other cultures and times. Fantasy and fiction make good past times.

Wednesday 24th

Make the most of the dreamy energy you are receiving. Your rulers both connect to the Moon, but Pluto needs you to get back on dry land and take the wheel again. Your career needs you to step up and show people what you are made of. How can you make the transition from dreams to solid reality?

Thursday 25th

Difficult energy between the Moon and planets in your family sector make it hard for you to concentrate. You may feel restricted and pulled in different directions. Mars and Pluto combine to give you the strength to fix on the job in hand. Don't have a tantrum.

Friday 26th

Venus has drifted into your creative sector. The ethereal mermaid will add beauty to anything you do now. She will also help a love interest take root. Stay focused on work and show compassion for colleagues. You may need to be more self-disciplined this evening when the Moon opposes Venus.

Saturday 27th

A beautiful Full Moon occurs in your social sector today. This will highlight where you may have been hard on yourself or been taken for granted by friendship groups. Perhaps you put in more than you get out. Perhaps you are the light by which others find their way.

Sunday 28th

The energy today is very earthy and grounding. You need to take advantage of this and do something to help yourself. A walk in nature, yoga, sex or eating good food will be satisfactory. Pluto and Mars are looking after you; you're assertive and in control.

MARCH

. . . .

Monday 1st

The Moon in your hidden sector suggests that you're trying
to justify your deepest thoughts. Family issues will be on your
mind as you attempt to cut through superficiality to find the
root of problems. The danger here is that you can over-analyse.
You don't need to be judge and jury.

Tuesday 2nd

You have a busy mind and will be pulling out all your old
resources and knowledge. Locked in thought, you may
be reminiscing and thinking of how you could have acted
better. Use these thoughts to help you grow in similar
future scenarios. Switch off and rest this evening.

Wednesday 3rd

The Moon has come back to your own sign. You may find
that there's some unrest bubbling up in your relationships or
your own shadow side. Venus and the Sun in your romantic
creative sector help you to work with this material in a way
which benefits you.

Thursday 4th

You're intensely Scorpian today. Mercury and Jupiter make your
thoughts and conversations huge and some people may find that
hard to deal with. You are looking to change something in your
life and others are feeling left behind. Neptune should help you
to see things from their point of view.

Friday 5th

It's possible that you feel a little touchy and anxious today. Mars opposes the Moon and you may feel protective about your own environment. Be careful how you converse with others today, as you may say something you wish you hadn't. You could have a 'Eureka!' moment with your family.

Saturday 6th

Emotionally, you're pulled back into thoughts of the past. Look at what you learned back then. Can you use it again now? Jupiter and Mercury are still together making intellectual conversations and genius thinking bigger than usual. This is an opportunity to birth something new.

Sunday 7th

This is a day where love overtures can be made gently to positive effect. A Sunday afternoon treat with a loved one may provide the perfect moment. Venus and Uranus connect to an outgoing Moon, meaning you could be in for a lovely surprise. Alternatively, you might make an irrational impulse purchase.

Monday 8th

Take today one step at a time. You must be responsible and adult. Conversations may also take on a serious tone. There's still a chance to woo the one you are falling for, but you must remember to stay safe and respect each other's boundaries. Merge with the other without being pushy.

Tuesday 9th

When the Moon meets Pluto today, you may feel a power struggle going on. This could come from within you. Maybe you have lost your courage. Use the energy from Mars to move forward bravely. Family matters might take up your time this evening. Share love and laughter with your tribe.

Wednesday 10th

The Sun meets Neptune today. This has the effect of burning away any illusions you have been harbouring in your creative sector. Remove the rose-tinted spectacles and take a good look at what is in front of you. Be wise and evaluate what you see with the greatest compassion.

Thursday 11th

The Moon and Mercury meet up. Your head and heart are having a discussion. Logic and reason are opposing your heartfelt emotions today. This is tough, so don't make any decisions and hold off voicing how you feel. This phase will pass soon; wait for clarity to come.

Friday 12th

Your creative self is jumpy and wants to express something. Try getting this down on paper, canvas or music. You have Uranus lending you his genius energy today; whatever you create will be electrified. You may have a breakthrough moment with a project you have previously struggled with.

Saturday 13th

Today there's a New Moon in your creative sector. This is an excellent time for you to set goals and intentions around something artistic, or even around a love interest. When the Moon meets Neptune, take a moment to be still and receive messages from your inner compass and find your true north.

Sunday 14th

Venus and Neptune meet. On the back of the New Moon, this is a wonderful day for love, beauty, inspiration and spiritual matters. You can bask in the beautiful energy and feel quite surreal. Don't waste it by drifting off; stay focused and get your creative head on.

Monday 15th

As the Moon shifts, so does the energy. The 'back to work' feeling is upon you, but you are motivated and cheerful. You have many chores to get through, but this will be easy. If you have time for yourself, check in with your body or maybe get a work-out.

Tuesday 16th

Today, you must be careful not to let your ego lead the way. Both the Sun and the Moon are connecting to Pluto in your communications sector. Pluto asks for change or endings, so think twice before offering advice or information to others. You desire to speak out but now isn't the time.

Wednesday 17th

You're overly romantic today. Mercury has moved into your creative sector and your mind will be busy and inquisitive. Be mindful that you do not go building castles in the sky. The Moon meets Uranus, making you edgy, shocking or rebellious. Direct that energy into something grounding.

Thursday 18th

Neptune and Venus combine to make you romantic and idealistic now. There's a figure in your family sector who doesn't approve. You may have to be pulled back down to earth and get a reality check. Don't go pushing boundaries, as they will backfire on you.

Friday 19th

Your mind is so busy that it's at bursting point. Mars is giving you the drive to push forward into deeper waters, but you may not be prepared for what you find. Check any finances owed or due to you, especially those that are tied up with another person.

Saturday 20th

Today is the Spring Equinox. This is a great time to pause and reflect on where you think you are going this year. Try not to get dragged into fantastical thinking and make sure that you keep all goals realistic. The Sun, now in your health and duties sector, asks you to be sensible.

Sunday 21st

Venus enters your health and duties sector. Whilst she's here, you're being taught to look after yourself better. Health is likely to be an issue now, even if that simply means checking your personal energy and saving some for yourself. Be warrior-like about your wellbeing.

Monday 22nd

Travel and higher education are on your mind. You desire to experience other cultures but aren't yet ready to leave the safety of your own home. Documentaries, cooking or study will help to ease that yearning. Sign up for something, now; you may surprise yourself and enjoy it very much.

Tuesday 23rd

Today you feel a tension between home and career. This may be difficult to reconcile. Mothers and fathers, or similar figures of authority, can come into conflict now. You may find that you dream of lost relatives or loved ones. Your inner-child and inner-parent need to have a talk.

Wednesday 24th

The Moon is in your fiery career sector. However, you may very well have trouble expressing yourself due to Mars and Mercury squaring off. Mars can make you run before you can walk and Mercury may give you unrealistic fantasies. Take time off and look after yourself with rest, pampering or good food.

Thursday 25th

The Sun and Venus are together in your health and duties sector, making it imperative that you don't over-task yourself today. You're valued for the work you put into helping others and being a guiding light, but right now you should be putting yourself first.

Friday 26th

Your energy picks up as Mars meets the point of fate in your intimacy sector. You may get an idea of something new which will excite and exhilarate you. Check all the facts before proceeding and do not go in all guns blazing. Get ready for a weekend with friends.

Saturday 27th

Today you may feel at a standstill. Perhaps your energy has crashed, just as you were wanting to be social and active. You may even be ill. Whatever the cause, be careful not to stretch yourself too thinly. If your social groups wish to engage, let them come to you for now.

Sunday 28th

A Full Moon lights up your darkest hidden sector today. This may feel very uncomfortable. You're used to delving around in your psyche, but today you may feel unexpected triggers. This could be a culmination of something that was started six months ago. Check back and see what it might be.

Monday 29th

You are much more together and focused now. Saturn and Mars are connecting to the Moon in your hidden sector, helping you to deal with any triggers responsibly. Only you know how far you can stretch; if you wish to stay private, then do so.

Tuesday 30th

This morning, the Moon drops into your sign and opposes Uranus. This can make you feel restless, but this isn't always a bad thing. Work it through and let something productive come of it. Mercury and Neptune meet. This strange combination will keep your mind busy with dreams, visions and inner guidance.

Wednesday 31st

You will get some idea of what Neptune and Mercury have been up to, now. Your heart will pull you in the right direction, even if just for a while. Follow that yearning; it's your inner compass re-calibrating. Family members may wonder what on Earth you are up to now.

APRIL

. . . .

Thursday 1st

Take a look around your home today. What needs to be recycled
or transformed? This could be a project that vitalises you and
spruces up your environment. Look at your bank balance
and check that there is nothing outstanding. There may be
subscriptions which you can now cancel.

Friday 2nd

There is a lot of lovely energy coming to you today. You may
be bringing back skills you have learned in the past or lovingly
letting go of unnecessary baggage. The Sun and Venus are helping
you to shed some dead weight and move on with a lighter load.
Could this be preparing you for something on the horizon?

Saturday 3rd

Mercury is at the final degrees of your creative sector. It's critical
that you speak openly to a love interest. This may be difficult to
do as your emotions are tied up in letting things go. When the
Moon shifts into your communication sector, this will be easier.
Do it this evening.

Sunday 4th

Mercury is now in your health and duties sector. This is the
beginning of the whole astrological chart and he appears to
be on a new mission. This will involve being good to yourself
as well as to others. Make plans to do what you want to do.
Surprise yourself.

Monday 5th

The Moon has her monthly meeting with Pluto. Have a talk with yourself about how it feels to reduce and transform what you have. This afternoon, family issues need your attention, and this may even be fun. Enjoy the diversity of your tribe and celebrate individuality with them.

Tuesday 6th

What might you have to learn from a family elder? Saturn represents old people, leaders and teachers. He may be harsh at times but has your best interests at heart. Watch out for a valuable lesson today. Venus and Mars are in harmony; intimacy and self-care are intertwined.

Wednesday 7th

At home, the love is shared around and there is harmony. Nurturing is at it's best today. When the Moon meets Jupiter, you will have a chance to think big and make a wish. Reach for the stars now. The collective of the family is highly favoured from this meeting.

Thursday 8th

You're feeling creative and romantic. Your self-expression is good, but you get drawn into negative thinking by remembering past issues. This could unsettle you, so stay focused on the present and get making pretty things or writing soft words. Genius thinking is brought to you by inspiration from relationships.

Friday 9th

You may find yourself over-thinking again. Mars in your intimacy sector is draining your energy. Try doing something active and getting out of your head for a while. When the Moon meets Neptune, there's a chance you'll have to surrender or sacrifice some of that energy for another cause, probably a love interest.

Saturday 10th

The Moon shifts into your health and duties sector and you should feel more energised. Venus and Mercury allow you to get on with your day with good cheer. This is approved of by Saturn and Jupiter, who act like elders in your tribe. They are proud of your achievements today.

Sunday 11th

This is a great time for your heart and head to have a talk. Ask yourself if you are following your own path or being a passenger on someone else's. The Moon has met Mercury and is trying to feel her way to Mercury's next mission for you.

Monday 12th

A New Moon in your health and duties sector gives you a great opportunity to make solid plans and intentions regarding how you take care of yourself and others. Venus and the Moon have a ladies' night and suggest a pamper session for you. Don't feel guilty about this.

Tuesday 13th

The Moon shifts into your relationship sector and meets Uranus. It's possible that you're provoked to boiling point and a row ensues. Extra energy from the Sun and Mars can fuel this conflict or turn it into energy worth using with a lover or business partner.

Wednesday 14th

Venus is at the final degree of your health and duties sector. Take a very good look at what she has taught you recently. It's imperative that you carry on being good to yourself, thus enabling your spare energy to be used elsewhere. Check in with your health now.

Thursday 15th

The Moon moves into your intimacy sector, just as Venus enters your relationship sector. This can be good news for a romantic relationship. Jupiter is looking on and sending his blessings for a lucky day. Mars is also with you today; as your ruler, he's responsible for your sex drive.

Friday 16th

Today you may need to pause before leaping into anything beyond your comfort zone. Keep both feet on the ground and consider all possibilities before edging your way gently into the unknown. Easy does it; if you have thought this through and take it slowly, you have nothing to fear.

Saturday 17th

The Moon meets Mars in your intimacy sector. He will armour you up and protect you when you walk unknown lands. Mercury is very excited about this, and connects to other planets to help you navigate this in your mind and to others in deep conversation.

Sunday 18th

Think about nurturing yourself today. The Moon in your travel sector requires that you feel safe and secure. Try a good book or documentary about a culture that piques your interest. Mercury has left you alone to gather new information. What will you find?

Monday 19th

Both the Sun and Mercury enter your relationship sector. Expect your closest relationships to heat up with a lot of chatter and inquiry. This may be the time you get to know someone better. It could also mean that you're opening up to someone you feel safe with. This is good news.

Tuesday 20th

There's a danger that you come across as a show-off or a bully today. Pluto is opposing the Moon, meaning that control issues or power struggles are likely. The Moon also squares off with Venus and Mercury. Be respectful and kind. Show off your best qualities, not your worst.

Wednesday 21st

You must have touched a raw spot with someone recently. The energy today is no better and still suggests that you've overstepped the mark. You will have to retrace your steps and discover the point where it all went wrong. Humble pie is on the menu tonight.

Thursday 22nd

This morning you may be licking your wounds and facing up to an authority figure. Apologise and retreat with your head bowed low. Mars is at the final degree of your intimacy sector, asking that you put things right before he moves. You can do this; the Sun and Mercury have your back.

Friday 23rd

Better energy arrives for the weekend. The Moon is in your social sector and connecting to Venus and Uranus. Love and surprise can be mixed, maybe an apology with a gift or a treat is in order. Venus loves to be wined and dined in your relationship sector.

Saturday 24th

Neptune is trying to call you away to a fantasy land, but you'll likely refuse the offer. It's far better to stay on firm ground today. Mercury meets Uranus and this can be temperamental. There will either be a row or a highly charged conversation with a lover which produces fruit.

Sunday 25th

Settle into your hidden sector for the rest of the weekend; you may need to spend some time alone. The time to process recent events is now. Words of love can be exchanged but they need to be within your boundaries and another's. Stay respectful and kind.

Monday 26th

Self-control keeps you out of trouble today. You desire to get your own way in a playful manner. Home comforts or forgotten favourite meals will satisfy you. Let your inner child be comforted today. Make a blanket tent and enjoy an ice-cream all to yourself.

Tuesday 27th

Today is your Full Moon. It comes with difficult connections to Uranus, Venus and Mercury in your relationship sector. You may just want to stay in your tent and be alone. This energy is asking for change, big change, and you're not prepared to do it. This will sneak up on you.

Wednesday 28th

Your secondary ruler, Pluto, turns retrograde today. This will occur in your communications sector. You must evaluate all issues regarding siblings, conversations, short trips and messages. How you get what you want and climb the corporate ladder will also be an issue now. You may need to step down a few rungs.

Thursday 29th

Breathe deeply and step outside. Imagine you're leaving a room of useless things and not coming back. Now, look around you. This is a good starting point to make your way slowly to where you want to be. You yearn for truth and the wider world now.

Friday 30th

The Sun meets Uranus today. This is like nuclear fusion and can produce highly unstable energy. How can you use this influence for the best, in your relationship sector? It may be sparks of a love affair or a loose cannon waiting to blow. Use it wisely.

MAY

· · · · · · · · · · · · · · · · ·

Saturday 1st

Your relationship sector is on fire. The Sun and Uranus are still causing eruptions of ego and will. The Moon hanging around in your communications sector means that you're emotionally invested in getting your message through. Speak from the heart and remain respectful and responsible.

Sunday 2nd

It's possible to rectify a poor situation today. Venus and Mercury are helping you to do your very best in saying how you feel to someone special. Watch out that you don't become passive-aggressive when the Moon meets Pluto. All is not lost if you are true to your word.

Monday 3rd

There's still a lot of tension in the air. However, if you base yourself in your home environment you may be able to ride it better. Behave like an adult and accept a truce if one is offered. You have the potential to spoil or correct something that has gone awry.

Tuesday 4th

Mercury flies into his home sign which, for you, is your soul-searching, intimate sector. You may be asking a lot of questions of yourself today. The Moon and Venus aren't communicating, and you may feel that you would rather spend time at home than with a lover.

Wednesday 5th

You desire to find the truth and stretch your borders out into the wider world. Time spent wondering 'what if' is pointless today, as you will receive no answers. The Moon shifts into your creative sector and brings a softer edge to your seeking. Listen to your heart now.

Thursday 6th

Jupiter sits at the final degree of your family sector. It's a good idea to think hard about recent events and how you are perceived by authority figures in your tribe. When the Moon meets Neptune later, you just want to switch off and be alone.

Friday 7th

Have you neglected your mundane duties? You now have the energy to get up-to-date and leave nothing outstanding. Venus helps you to be considerate of others whilst Pluto in retrograde ensures that changes are made for the better. You may need to be somewhat ruthless today.

Saturday 8th

Make sure that your schedule is correct and your day is planned well. There may be many jobs to do for others and no time for yourself. You will have to choose who you spend your time with today. Remember: duty first, fun later. Relax with a loved one this evening.

Sunday 9th

Venus follows Mercury into your intimacy sector. This is good news, as she will help you to explore the mysteries and cycles of life with compassion. Here she can ask all the right questions and restore harmony if there is an upset. You will feel grateful for the love you receive today.

Monday 10th

You are stirred by the Moon's monthly meeting with Uranus. Mars is also connecting well, so it's likely that you can turn this evening into a lively, emotional reunion. Mars wants to protect those he loves and you are won over by this energy. Protect and be protected in return.

Tuesday 11th

A New Moon in your opposite sign is your chance to set new goals regarding relationships that are important to you. Think of how you can put down roots and be more grounded. You may want to consider activities which help you connect with your body and the land.

Wednesday 12th

As the Moon slips into your intimacy sector, she meets Venus and they are best friends again. Your heart's desires can now be gently pursued. The volatile planets Mars and Uranus combine well to give you an exciting and energetic thrill. All is well in the house of love today.

Thursday 13th

Let your head and heart have a long discussion today. You have much to think about and you need to process it so that you fully understand your place. You may be exchanging ideas, concepts and beliefs that are strange to you but interest you nonetheless.

Friday 14th

Jupiter enters your creative sector. Despite his retrograde period, this stay will be beneficial to you and your artistic or love projects. Expect everything to get larger than life, but try to keep one foot on the ground in this dreamy part of your chart. Seek your holy grail or your muse now.

Saturday 15th

The Moon hits watery territory, which you're familiar with. Your emotions need nurturing and protecting. Here is where you can let yourself dream and fly. Maybe a visit to a foreign land by way of a dinner, a documentary or reading will suffice. Enjoy broadening your horizons a little.

Sunday 16th

Today, you're driven to make your taste for the unknown a reality. It's a good time to plan a vacation when the Moon meets Mars. Get you trekking boots on and go out for a stroll. Go beyond your comfort zone and see how it feels for you.

Monday 17th

Both the Sun and Moon connect to Pluto. This will feel like persuasion, coercion or passive aggression. Let a lover lead the way and put your fears to one side. Stretching your boundaries just a little is essential for your soul growth. Make sure that you take one step at a time.

Tuesday 18th

Someone is watching you in the workplace today. Make every move count and be ultra-professional. Saturn is doing an appraisal on how well you perform. He's making sure that you're giving it all you've got and shining in all your glory. Own it; you deserve it.

Wednesday 19th

Keep strutting your stuff and maintain a quality performance at work. Jupiter is watching that you are honest and going the extra mile if you're asked. He also reminds you to whistle while you work and spread good cheer. Others will follow your lead today.

Thursday 20th

You may wish to check your schedule and get ready for the weekend. Friends are calling and checking in with you. There could be someone who needs your help or simply your presence. Be very aware that some connections drain your energy. Venus is reminding you of this right now.

Friday 21st

The Sun has shifted into your intimacy sector. This move will bring added warmth to an area that always seems cold and detached to you. It will also shine through the darkest tunnels in order for you to find the gold you're looking for. Happy hunting.

Saturday 22nd

Mercury and Neptune may have a conundrum for you today. Neptune's mists float over your thinking and you simply cannot find a logical answer to a problem. Indeed, it's probably hard for you to find clarity in anything today. This influence will soon pass; be patient.

Sunday 23rd

That old teacher planet, Saturn, turns retrograde in your family sector. He is firm but fair and his retrogrades ask that you go over old ground and make sure you have understood what is required of you. This is the time to check in with elders in your family, too.

Monday 24th

You are back in your body and feel like yourself again. The Moon has landed in your sign and you're on top form. Unfortunately, this also means that the monthly opposition to Uranus is here and you may be temperamental or excitable. Use this energy to have some fun with your lover.

Tuesday 25th

Watery energy from Mars and Neptune can make you over-emotional, but this isn't new territory to you. A poor connection to Saturn in retrograde lets you know that you must not wallow in it. Get up, wipe your tears or – at the very least – write about it.

Wednesday 26th

Today you will see a Full Moon in your finances and worth sector. What has come to fruition regarding these issues? There may be a financial investment from the past that you have forgotten about that now comes in handy. Get that vacation booked now; don't you deserve it?

Thursday 27th

Today's energy can be a little tricky to handle. Money is an issue, as Venus and Mercury both oppose the Moon. These are all in sectors concerning finances. Check obligations shared with another as they may have expired. Venus and Mercury are both connected to money, so this is important.

Friday 28th

You may have some tasks to complete before checking out for the weekend. Use today to go through your planner and ensure that nothing is outstanding. This is a day to work steadily and impress someone with your stamina. Mercury goes retrograde tomorrow, so check everything twice.

Saturday 29th

On the first day of his retrograde, Mercury turns to Venus and asks her to take care of things in your intimacy sector. She can retain balance and harmony here. Both of your rulers connect to the Moon today; this can be empowering or unsettling if you are sensitive.

Sunday 30th

This is an easy day for you, so why not use it to unwind and do something for yourself? The Moon is in your family sector but that does not mean you need to spend the day with them. Ask for a respectful space to simply do your own thing today.

Monday 31st

The Moon meets Saturn and you come face to face with a responsibility you may have neglected. You will feel like a schoolchild being reprimanded. Never mind. Use this opportunity to learn a lesson and up your game for next time. This is what Saturn retrogrades are all about.

JUNE

· · · · · · · · · · · · · · · · ·

Tuesday 1st

If you're extra-creative or romantic today, make the most of it. The Moon joins Jupiter freshly in this sector and connects to Venus. Many blessings can come your way today, all you need to do is make a wish. With the Sun in its current position, you cannot go wrong.

Wednesday 2nd

Venus drops into your travel sector and becomes the eternal nurturer. She will feed you what your soul desires, now. You may feel a short crisis of conscience and hesitate to make progress today, but rest assured that you are moving forward. This influence will pass very quickly.

Thursday 3rd

The Moon meets up with Neptune, giving you a rest-stop to catch your breath and look around you. You may be feeling vulnerable right now. Your emotions are reacting to the changes Pluto is making for you. You must learn to let something go or have it clutter up your forward growth.

Friday 4th

Mercury retrograde is playing tricks with you. It's likely that you're reconsidering something. You don't yet have all the information you need to make a decision, so it's perhaps best to wait until the retrograde is over. Venus and Jupiter are continuing to shower you with blessings today.

Saturday 5th

Today there's a lot of difficult energy and you will probably feel this intensely, as it involves your two rulers. The best thing you can do is to have a day in your blanket tent and take care of your own needs. Don't get pulled into other people's dramas.

Sunday 6th

It's safe to come out and interact with other humans now. The Moon is in your relationship sector and has Venus and Jupiter connecting lovingly again. If you're in the mood, today can be great for love relationships. You should feel truly connected and cared for. Enjoy this energy

Monday 7th

You must be very respectful of people's boundaries today. Uranus is visited by the Moon and that unstable energy doesn't need much to tip it over boiling point. Saturn is watching how you respond to your lover today. Play nicely and you will be respected in return.

Tuesday 8th

As the Moon shifts, deeper issues niggle at you. Your rulers are asking that you look at parenting, responsibility, nurturing, legacy and inheritances. There may be some skeletons in the closet waiting to be aired. Be sure to check your bank balance as you may see some discrepancies.

Wednesday 9th

You may be wondering just where you're heading this year. This monthly meeting with the point of fate has the Moon pulling your emotions to an unknown future. How far would you like to go? Would you rather stay safe and feel secure? Or are you ready to take a risk?

Thursday 10th

A New Moon in your intimacy sector has come just at the right time. Try not to overthink and complicate your thinking, as the Moon will shortly meet Mercury in retrograde in his own sign. Get your goals and intentions straight in your head but keep them to yourself for a while.

Friday 11th

Mercury has nothing to say today as he is in the heat of the Sun. It's your job to listen for messages from your dreams and from whispers, gossip or other sources. Filter the useful stuff for later. Mars enters your career sector, so expect to be extra-productive in the workplace now.

Saturday 12th

The Moon and Venus meet up in your travel sector. Why not enjoy a Saturday visiting new locations? There's a chance you will fall in love with them and will wish to return often. Spoil yourself with good food. A family favourite from childhood will go down well.

Sunday 13th

The Moon meets Mars in your career sector and passes on Venus' love. What Venus wants, Mars gets, so here's a chance to use your ruler to help you shine in the workplace. Nurturers and protectors can combine to make the best spiritual warriors who are driven by compassion today.

Monday 14th

You may be tested at work today. The Moon is making difficult connections to Uranus and Saturn. It's likely that you will try to fight a losing battle or let your temper get the better of you. This will not go down too well and you will have to retreat with your wounds.

Tuesday 15th

Saturn and Uranus are squaring off. This could signify a conflict between elders in your family and instability in your relationship sector. Perhaps everybody wants your time today. There is no easy way to deal with this, as someone will get angry and have a tantrum. Good luck.

Wednesday 16th

Your social groups require your presence today. Check in with your friends or online acquaintances as there may someone who needs your words of wisdom. You make a good listener but be careful not to give all your energy away. Keep some for yourself and give yourself a small treat.

Thursday 17th

It's likely that you experience arguments or misunderstandings in your social sector today. You will take this to heart and brood over it. Remember that Mercury is in retrograde and the Moon sits opposite Neptune today, so detach from the drama and wait until these connections shift for a clearer view.

Friday 18th

This morning the Moon enters your private and hidden sector. It connects to both your rulers, so you may need to do some introspection and justify your actions in some way. This will cause you some distress but will ultimately make more room for better things to come in.

Saturday 19th

Spend some time alone today. Your inner thoughts may be troubling you. Try to switch off and do something you enjoy. Read a book, watch a TV show or connect to spirit. Too much thinking time always gets you into trouble; you must change your perspective or distract yourself.

Sunday 20th

The Moon comes back to your sign today. However this only serves to make you more Scorpian than usual. You may experience feelings of jealousy or loss of personal power. The Moon isn't in a good position with your rulers but will shift quickly and you should feel better.

Monday 21st

The Summer Solstice is here, and the longest day brings with it Jupiter turning retrograde. Use this day to celebrate your gains this year. It's possible to dream and surrender to your lover today. Be mindful of personal boundaries and all will be well as Uranus can make you restless.

Tuesday 22nd

Mercury turns direct today and you can now revisit any plans you put off a few weeks ago. Watery energy from the Moon in your sign, Venus and Neptune can make this an emotional day. You're used to this and can channel this energy into something creative.

Wednesday 23rd

An outgoing Moon asks that you look at what you value around you. You may wish to declutter or renovate in your home. A new haircut or item of clothing will also suffice. Issues between men and women may surface. Watch out for passive aggression in your communications.

Thursday 24th

Today, there's a Full Moon in your communications sector. This will illuminate anything you have been working on steadily for the last six months. Look to your siblings, as they may require your attention now, too. Watch that you aren't fooled by insincere romantic notions today.

Friday 25th

Neptune turns retrograde now. This heralds a time where you may not get clarity on your creative or romantic projects. You will need to learn to surrender to the natural flow of life or change your mindset. Looking at things from a different perspective can be rewarding and brighten up your artistic endeavours.

Saturday 26th

A family day may be just what you need today. Is it time to clear the air and enjoy each other's company? You may resist this at first, but you will have fun by afternoon. Changes or endings may need to be made and this will not please someone. Prepare for some inevitable tension or fallout.

Sunday 27th

Venus makes her way into your career sector and will show you how to lead like a boss. Her compassion and harmonising qualities will be useful in the coming month. Your family sector may experience some tension and you may need to use mediation skills right now.

Monday 28th

Celebrate your uniqueness with the people who know you best. Your family of origin can be a source of much laughter, today. The Moon shifts to your creative sector and meets Jupiter in retrograde. Where you usually may think too big in this area, you now find that you are trimming away the unnecessary.

Tuesday 29th

Take some time to assess and evaluate how you are doing in your romance and artistic projects. Are you really expressing yourself from the heart? How are you showing up? You may need to check in with yourself and make sure that you are not wearing any masks.

Wednesday 30th

The Moon squares off with Mercury in your intimacy sector. Romance and deep concepts are just not in sync today. When the Moon meets Neptune, you will be unable to think this through. No need to get to the bottom of it right now; sleep on it. Rest will help to make things clearer.

JULY
. . . .

Thursday 1st

Even though you're ready to tick off a few things in your task list today, you could be lacking in energy. Mars opposes Saturn and this can feel like a dead weight. You may also feel that you need to go the extra mile, but it exhausts you. Put yourself first for now; you can't give to others what you are in need of yourself.

Friday 2nd

Communications are lively today. You may be putting forward a new business plan or researching a topic which is deep and mysterious. A busy mind will keep you from worrying about superficial issues. Shop for healthy foods for the weekend; your immune system may be in need of some support, and nourishing yourself will do you no harm.

Saturday 3rd

This afternoon, spend time with a lover or person you truly admire. There is much to be learned from an authority figure or spiritual leader. Pull back a little and do some grounding activities such as taking a walk, meditation or gardening. Pluto is asking you to switch up your routine.

Sunday 4th

Today might bring some tension with a loved one. The Moon is making poor connections to the celestial lovers Venus and Mars, both of whom are in your career sector. Uranus joins the party and will push buttons until the tension is released. Do not overstep boundaries today. Remember to be respectful.

Monday 5th

The Sun has moved sufficiently away from Uranus to work together nicely. This is good energy for brainstorming or planning trips to foreign lands. A lover may appreciate being involved, as you can dream and visualise together. Two head are better than one today. Remember to play nicely and reach for the sky.

Tuesday 6th

In your intimacy sector, the Moon squares off with Jupiter. Romance is not on the agenda today. You may find that shared visions are showing up vital flaws. Mercury and Neptune are not helping here, as your need for logic and reason clashes with another's idealistic intangible plans.

Wednesday 7th

Thoughts become clearer now. There is more harmony between men and women. Willpower and egos are in sync and can come together for a common goal. Venus and Mars are leading the way as compassionate warriors in your career sector. Don't overdo it; Saturn is watching that you don't abuse power.

Thursday 8th

The Moon and Mercury meet up in Mercury's own sign. Rational thinking will win over emotions today. There might be a pull towards fantasy, but you can overcome this. This afternoon you're more inclined to stay within your comfort zone and research from your own home.

. . . .

Friday 9th

It's possible for you to think outside the box today. A helping hand from your relationship sector uses Uranus' genius thinking to provide you with an unusual solution. This will please you, as it protects your personal boundaries whilst helping you step into the unknown. Be open to possibilities.

Saturday 10th

A New Moon in your travel sector is the chance you need to simultaneously expand your horizons and feel at home. Perhaps you have found a holiday destination where you're comfortable and yourself. This may be a past life showing you another place you can call home.

Sunday 11th

Mercury spends his last day in your intimacy sector. He wants to know the ins and outs of everything here. Make sure that you have the information you require about intense or taboo topics, or choose to leave it alone. Your career calls as the Moon shifts and enters this sector.

Monday 12th

This is a beautiful day for co-operation in the workplace. The Moon meets both Venus and Mars, who are getting closer. You may find love today or make an important working relationship. Mars gets what Venus wants and she likes money. Maybe you can ask for a raise now.

Tuesday 13th

Mars and Venus have met. Sparks are flying and the air is electric. They are powerful co-leaders in this area and can be an example to all. There may be a celebration today, during which you can get together with your social groups. There will be much to talk about.

Wednesday 14th

Surprises from your relationship sector will be more than satisfactory today. The Mars and Venus meet-up is still happening, and this fills your soul with a divine purpose. Have you had a light bulb moment? Have you suddenly decided on a career change or a new direction? Is this your vocation in life?

Thursday 15th

Now is the time to sit alone and process your most recent epiphanies. The Moon dips into your hidden sector, where you spend time weighing everything up and finding justification. Neptune is having connections from the Sun and Moon; you can dream logically with some hope thrown in.

Friday 16th

Mercury is sending you messages from your travel sector. He may be sending you words of doubt and discouragement. He acts as the devil on your shoulder, but this is your own self-talk; don't listen. Note it and how it makes you feel but don't take it as gospel truth.

Saturday 17th

Your rational private mind is connecting to Venus and Mars. You wonder how your leadership qualities can change your small part of the world. Pluto is playing tricks with you and asking you to let something go once and for all. This is necessary, although you may also find it upsetting.

Sunday 18th

The Moon is in your sign and opposes Uranus. You may feel extra-stubborn today and do your own thing, regardless of good advice. You know your own boundaries best but will overstep them when it suits you. This can have a negative effect today; proceed with caution.

Monday 19th

It's now you wanting to make changes. Neptune and Pluto are bewitching you today, but remember that these two outer planets are in retrograde and it isn't wise to make major life decisions right now. Your finances need to be looked at this evening. Have you over-spent recently?

Tuesday 20th

You're thinking about the past and how restricted you may have been. Your desire to explore and see the wider world has been blocked by your home and financial situations. Make a point of rectifying this as you are on to bigger and better things. Security first, then fun.

Wednesday 21st

Once again, Mars and Venus appeal to your emotional body. This time, it's in the area of your possessions and values. Take a look at your home environment and decide what you really need. Maybe it's time to think about a declutter and restoring harmony in your home.

Thursday 22nd

The Sun enters your career sector as Venus leaves it. The spotlight is on you. The Sun is in its own sign and is super powerful here. You may wish to put your career advancement into action. Venus will spread the love and harmony within your friendship groups, now.

Friday 23rd

In your communication sector, the Moon meets Pluto. If there is ever a time to declutter and lighten your load, it's now. You're climbing a mountain with baby steps, so don't take on any more weight. If you're already halfway up, check in with others who can help you advance.

Saturday 24th

A bright Full Moon in your family sector illuminates your tribe and celebrates the geniuses, the oddballs and quirky characters you have grown up with. As the Moon meets Saturn, take time to visit an elderly relative and listen to their stories. You may learn something.

Sunday 25th

Be careful today. Your two rulers are not well connected, and you may see tempers flare. Conversations can be misunderstood between men and women or opposing figures, and you may see passive-aggressive behaviour. Mars and Uranus are in this mix, making it a volatile day all around. Have a Sunday in bed, if you can. It might just be easier.

Monday 26th

Jupiter waits for the Moon to visit today. He's retrograde and at the beginning of your creative sector. You may be feeling sorry for yourself and want to hide away. Alternatively, your plans to merge and socialise might take a different turn and you could end up taking on a duty.

Tuesday 27th

Today, the Moon meets dreamy Neptune, who is busy covering romantic issues in a shroud of mystery. You may not get to the bottom of this one for a while. Simply go with the flow but keep one foot on the shore. A little surreal fun won't hurt you.

Wednesday 28th

Mercury now joins the office party in your career sector. If you're in areas such as research or intelligence, you can expect to be extra busy with him here. Watch out for workplace gossip and stay away from bullying behaviour. You may be super-efficient or too involved in other people's dramas.

Thursday 29th

Mars and Jupiter have a stand-off today. They're both at final degrees in your work and family sectors. You may have to choose where your energy goes as both areas require it. When Mars shifts, he rallies the troops of your social sector and organises rigorous group activities.

Friday 30th

It's time for a weekend with a lover or a special person. You could also spend money and time and treat yourself to a solo adventure. It's possible that you're in for a lively weekend, so maybe take a rest today to prepare yourself for a party or two.

Saturday 31st

The Moon is making poor connections today. You will probably find that you just cannot say the right thing to anyone. Messages may get mixed up, delayed or misunderstood. One saving grace is that Venus in your social sector still wants you to have a fun time this evening. Just think carefully when it comes to what and how you communicate.

AUGUST
· · · · · · · · · · · · · · · · ·

Sunday 1st

Once again, the Moon meets Uranus in your relationship sector. To avoid unnecessary tension, your job today is to listen to someone else letting off steam. Mercury is in the heat of the Sun, being silent. Take your cue from him and use active listening skills with compassion.

Monday 2nd

There will be a battle of wills around you. Your drive and emotions aren't in sync, and you may need to rein yourself in. The Sun in your career sector is facing off with the teacher planet, Saturn. Don't let your ego get the better of you; listen to those in charge.

Tuesday 3rd

Today you're questioning the meaning of your life, your status and where you are headed. This is all good stuff, as it allows you to evaluate the year so far and decide on a path of progression. Look to people you admire who can help you move on.

Wednesday 4th

Your mind is busy with concepts you may not fully understand. Superficiality doesn't interest you; it never does. You need a more intense connection. Talking about this with family may help, but it could cause problems if discussed with a romantic interest. You may shock someone with your thoughts.

Thursday 5th

There's gentle energy for you to access and take comfort in. The Moon's in your travel sector and you desire to find safety and security. Mars, your ruler, is working to equip you with all the details you need to be brave and strong enough to venture out. Together, they might be preparing you for something.

Friday 6th

Get advice, or at least some solid information, from your social groups today. Your lines of enquiry may prove fruitful and lead you on to a course of study or a short trip within your comfort zone. Someone may be too pushy and encourage you to go beyond your limits.

Saturday 7th

This morning, the Moon shifts into your carer sector and you step up your game. This outward energy asks you to shine your divine light into your society and let people know you're serious. You are admired more than you think; people need your light to keep shining.

Sunday 8th

A New Moon in your career sector lets you plant the seeds you wish to manifest regarding your progression and growth. You can be so assertive and definitive about this that you shock people who think they know you well. Play by the rules and you could win this race.

Monday 9th

When the Moon meets Mercury in your career sector, you find that your heart is telling your head what it desires. You may feel stupid discussing this with an elder or boss, but this is the way you'll process this possible big life change. Arm yourself with knowledge.

Tuesday 10th

The Moon meets Mars today and you are emotionally invested in attaining your goals. Mars is driven and has no time for fancy notions. Make mind maps, write a checklist, read reviews and make a plan. Your conscience wishes you to dream a little, but it's unlikely that you'll be able to find the time.

Wednesday 11th

When Venus hosts the Moon, you have a yearning to be of service to others, but this is not in alignment with your goals today. Free yourself from thoughts of martyrdom and learn to let things pass through you. You may help people, but remember to help yourself first. Mercury enters your social sector now.

Thursday 12th

You have much to think about. Spend time with your deepest thoughts and listen to your inner voice. Find it within yourself to aim for what excites you, as this is what can give you a strong sense of direction. Conversations with your social groups can offer you support when doing your introspection.

Friday 13th

When your mind is full of justifications, ask yourself if you are actually making excuses not to move onwards in life. You may have a moment of feeling stuck, but will realise that a change needs to be made. The Sun in your career sector is also supporting your inner thoughts.

Saturday 14th

You're more at ease with yourself now, as the Moon has landed in your sign. Your energy and drive to succeed have returned. A teacher, boss or elder in your family may try to restrict you and be negative about your plans. Talk them through your thoughts and they may understand.

Sunday 15th

Step away from the drama you may experience in your relationship sector today as it will drain you. Look instead to be creative and romantic. You can persuade someone to come down off their high horse and celebrate your visions with you. Just don't risk things by pushing them too far.

Monday 16th

Venus glides into your deepest thoughts now and will bring beauty and harmony your way. If you had any doubts before, Venus will smooth them over. Conversations with others can be fraught today, as the Moon is squaring off with both Mercury and Mars. Pause and be kind before speaking.

Tuesday 17th

Today has relatively easy energy for you but you must refrain from drifting off into fantasy land. Neptune is calling, but you can use this energy another way. Put yourself in someone else's shoes today and look at things from a different perspective. You may then appreciate them more.

Wednesday 18th

Your spoken words are not aligned with your innermost thoughts today. Why is that? Are you afraid of something? You don't need to rush into anything, especially if it results in you putting your guard up. If you are pressured, take one step at a time and achieve small goals at your own pace. Small progress is still better than no progress.

Thursday 19th

Restless Uranus goes retrograde today. You may feel the Earth move almost literally in your relationship sector. Mercury and Mars add fuel to the fire from your social groups; you will likely see arguments and disagreements with friends. The Moon connects well to these planets, so you will likely find yourself as a bystander when it all erupts.

Friday 20th

Open your eyes and you may see a truth that has been hiding from you in your family sector. The Sun opposes retrograde Jupiter and shows up any injustices in your tribe. Manipulation or power struggles will be evident today. Mind that your words are kind and honest.

Saturday 21st

The Moon in your family sector connects to newly retrograde Uranus. The usual rebelliousness of these two areas can turn nasty. Someone isn't toeing the line or acting out. This will also involve your love relationships, so think outside the box for a peace-keeping solution.

Sunday 22nd

A second Full Moon in your family sector means that if you did not catch the cues before, you surely will now. This Moon meets Jupiter and so this situation may be larger than you think. Shortly afterwards, the Moon moves onto softer waters and you may need to forgive, forget and move on.

Monday 23rd

The Sun slipped into your social sector without being noticed yesterday. You'll see some late summer fun with your groups being presented. A gentle, creative Moon may make you feel vulnerable as a feisty opposition from your social sector challenges it. You don't have to rise to this. Remember that.

Tuesday 24th

Today can be rather confusing for you. The Moon meets dreamy Neptune, who isn't letting you focus on your creative and romantic pursuits. Mercury is shouting his mouth off with ideas and directions, but you cannot hear him clearly. This presents difficult energy that you will just have to ride.

Wednesday 25th

Mercury and Neptune are at it again. Now that the Moon has shifted into your health and duties sector, you may just be able to hear Mercury's messages. Make a note of them and return to them when the energy is right. Today you have tasks to tick off your list.

Thursday 26th

There's something niggling you. Is there a chore or job that you must finish by today? You must look at your to-do list and decide which jobs hold priority. Something may be expiring soon; don't miss this, as it may still hold some value.

Friday 27th

Settle down and prepare for a weekend of spoiling yourself with a loved one. A solo treat will also suffice. Do something grounding such as walking, yoga or gardening. Maybe put down some solid foundations and begin building a relationship that is strong and solid. Try to be practical.

Saturday 28th

As she does every month, the Moon meets Uranus. This time, however, it's also receiving blessings from Venus, so you may be able to use this unstable energy to create or invent something innovative. Mars also connects, so you could be breaking ground in new ways.

Sunday 29th

Today you know just the right thing to say to someone special. You may woo a new lover or solidify your relationship with a current one. Either way, you have the gift of the gab and can seduce anyone. Make this a fine ending to the weekend and talk into the small hours.

Monday 30th

Mercury takes a dive into your hidden sector today. This may herald a time when you do a lot of introspection. Your innermost thoughts will not be kept a secret from Mercury as he roots around the darkest depths of your psyche and discovers pearls. This is soul work at its finest.

Tuesday 31st

You may feel a little edgy today and this could be due to Mercury's expedition. Mars wants you to pay attention to all the details, but Neptune is masking everything and you simply cannot grasp anything solid. This phase will soon pass, so just try to stick with it.

SEPTEMBER

· · · · · · · · · · · · · · · · ·

Wednesday 1st

If you feel over-emotional today, know that this is Mercury
rooting around in your subconscious. You will experience past
traumas surfacing to be healed. These are likely to be situations
or conditioning from your childhood and will trigger feelings of
safety. Let them rise and acknowledge them.

Thursday 2nd

Venus attempts to restore harmony to help you process
uncomfortable thoughts; this won't be easy. You're more
inclined to go with the energy from your ruler, Mars. If you
feel tired today, rest. If you feel angry, retreat. If you need time
alone, take it. Today's the right time to listen and take notice of
your own needs.

Friday 3rd

The Moon connects to Mars, indicating that you should
currently have the strength and courage to open yourself to the
healing process. Pluto opposes the Moon but is also your ruler,
so use his transformative energy to find the good in something.
You may see some sort of closure now; this will be good.

Saturday 4th

The Moon shifts into your career sector and you understand
that you now have to show an example to others. You're
beginning to see how the tears in your psyche let your light
through. You are strong and courageous. Let off some steam
safely, if you need to.

Sunday 5th

It's possible that you experience a confrontation with an elder in your family. Maybe there's something from the past that needs to be revisited. You should know just how to handle this, as Mercury and Saturn combine to make you articulate this situation in an adult and respectful manner.

Monday 6th

A little help from your wider groups or friendships should bring you some peace. You can sit comfortably and assess the past and future together, finding it easier to draw a line under a past experience. Be careful that your energy doesn't attract people who will suck it all from you.

Tuesday 7th

A New Moon in your social sector will get you looking at your health, energy and how you serve others. You must discern surrender from sacrifice and not be a scapegoat today. When the Moon meets your ruler, you pick up speed and resolve to put more effort into maintaining your health.

Wednesday 8th

The Moon drops into your hidden sector and you may ruminate on recent revelations. Use today to restore balance to your heart and mind. You may wish to consult a friend who can support your inner work and guide you to the next step. Inner development and healing will come easier today.

Thursday 9th

The Moon meets Mercury. Your heart and head have a conference and, although you understand that Mercury is dredging up uncomfortable material, you've yet to acknowledge the pearls he's also found. Try to keep your emotions away from any decision making which you may need to do.

Friday 10th

The Moon meets Venus just before she slips into your sign. This is beneficial energy, as the two of them together can soothe your pain with feminine wisdom and intuition. Avoid listening to male authority figures today; females will make more sense and heal your inner wounds.

Saturday 11th

With the Moon in your sign, it is possible that you become more secretive and mysterious. You are brooding over recent discoveries, but in a positive way. There's opposition from your relationship sector with Uranus, but you can ignore this and concentrate on coming back to your personal power.

Sunday 12th

Once again you need to use your ruler, Mars, to get you through the day. Family members or spiritual leaders may antagonise you, but Mars will keep you driven and assertive. Staying focused and on task will buoy you up and prevent you from going under.

Monday 13th

An outgoing, adventurous Moon now lets you see that deep inner work is rewarding and self-serving. You can justify this with yourself now. Neptune is attempting to keep your creative mind shrouded in fog, but you're parting it and getting through easily. This is creative work after all.

Tuesday 14th

You get a helping hand from the Sun today as it opposes Neptune and burns away some mist. Look around you, especially in your creative and romantic pursuits. What might you be seeing that you have missed previously? Recognise that these small steps count when climbing this mountain called self-discovery.

Wednesday 15th

Mars now marches into your hidden sector and your personal energy picks up. You will be determined to get to the bottom of anything else that Mercury brings up for you. Dedication to doing your inner work is highly commendable and, with your ruler by your side, you cannot fail.

Thursday 16th

When the Moon meets Pluto in your communications sector, you just know that endings or permanent changes you have made recently have been good for you. You are satisfied with your own progress. This afternoon you can relax and spend time with your loved ones and family of origin.

Friday 17th

Venus in your sign is helping you love yourself and get what you need. However, she does it in the manner of a seductress. Uranus in your opposite sector of relationships sees it as selfishness and has a tantrum. You must put yourself first and protect your own energy. Be kind and responsible.

Saturday 18th

A family day can prove relaxing for you. Fun and frolics with your wacky, unique tribe will lift your spirits. Jupiter meets the Moon and, although retrograde, he blesses you with laughter and joy. Do as he suggests and do something to let your hair down today.

Sunday 19th

Venus and Uranus appear to connect better today. The Moon in your dreamy creative sector holds them both at arms-length. A day with a lover will be sweet and exciting. If you have the energy, it can be very sexy too. Surprise each other with asking for what you desire.

Monday 20th

A romantic Full Moon in your creative sector lights the way for connection with like-minded souls. The Moon meets Neptune, you can surrender to the flow of a relationship. Listening to evocative music will be a good activity. Find your muse.

Tuesday 21st

As the Moon shifts, you become more assertive. There may be a list of jobs for you to do but you're happy to oblige. Try not to become emotionally attached, as there's a danger of being let down or feeling burnt out. Don't add any unnecessary chores to your list.

Wednesday 22nd

Tonight, the Autumn Equinox arrives, and day and night are equal lengths. As this is marked by the Sun moving into your hidden sector, you may wish to pause and reflect today. If it's possible, do nothing. Make no judgement calls or plans, simply be in the moment.

Thursday 23rd

This is unlikely to be an easy day. Conversations may be fraught with tension. Venus and Uranus are still opposing each other, putting your needs in direct conflict with those of another. It's best to say nothing or avoid a certain person altogether, if it's indeed possible. Otherwise, you may come to blows.

Friday 24th

The Moon joins Uranus and you're close to boiling point. You're emotionally invested in something which you are reluctant to let go. It's possible that this is your own shadow material surfacing and you may be projecting onto someone who doesn't deserve it. Breathe deeply, take a step back if you need to, and try to cut others some slack.

Saturday 25th

The energy today is calmer and you'll find it easier to pull yourself together. Mercury goes retrograde tomorrow, so use today to back up all your devices and double-check travel plans. This retrograde may be tough on you, as it will be in your hidden sector and will throw up a lot of debris.

Sunday 26th

You begin this retrograde of Mercury with the Moon in your intimacy sector. Emotionally, you're receiving useful energy from the Sun and Mars, but Saturn is telling you not to go too far with a special person. Respect personal boundaries now. Check on finances you share with another; they may need a tweak.

Monday 27th

Trying to get clarity on situations from your intimacy and creative sectors will not be easy. You can push as much as you like for answers, but you will not be told the whole truth. This is Neptune hiding things again. Try not to get frustrated; perhaps wait until the Moon shifts and try again.

Tuesday 28th

Your mind is busy with inquiry today. You want to know everything about subjects that most people avoid talking about. The Moon connects to Mercury retrograde and you may be going over old ground in an effort to understand these concepts better. This may exhaust you. Take the time to step back and look at things from other perspectives.

Wednesday 29th

Today you'll probably desire some home comforts and security. Favourite foods or exotic flavours may evoke memories of childhood when you felt safe. You may contemplate your own comfort zones and where you best feel nurtured. Time alone is time well spent. Treat yourself to something you can enjoy by on your own.

Thursday 30th

Revel in the great water energy that the planets offer. Go to the ocean, take a salt bath, be poetic and emotional. You're fully at home when merging with spiritual groups or meditating now. Let your words flow and create a masterpiece of art. Be romantic and hopeful.

OCTOBER

....

Friday 1st

Today, you're likely to be a force to be reckoned with. The Moon in your career sector brings your leadership skills to everyone's eyes. You can be ruthless and make any necessary adjustments needed. There is stuff surfacing from your psyche, and you're prepared to deal with it head-on.

Saturday 2nd

People who are closely related to you will frown upon your boldness right now. Let them; you're working towards being authentic in all that you do. That is bound to upset someone. Venus in your sign is helping you to value yourself and build your self-esteem. Work with her.

Sunday 3rd

You'll likely find yourself wishing to spend time with friends or simply engage on social media with your wider interest groups. Mercury retrograde is still excavating your deepest self, so be prepared for something big to come up today when he contacts Jupiter. Conditioning and family issues may be the subject of revelations today.

Monday 4th

You may struggle a little today when the Moon opposes Neptune. This is a position where you contemplate your role within friendship groups. Think about how you serve others and how you sometimes sacrifice your values to keep the peace. Hold off from agreeing to anything, even if it's simply asking someone to come back tomorrow for an answer.

Tuesday 5th

Are you being observant? Stay alert to people who may try to manipulate you, as this will throw you off-track. It's OK to say no. You have Venus cheerleading for you as you stand up for yourself lovingly. This afternoon, you become more introspective and need time alone.

Wednesday 6th

A New Moon occurs in your hidden sector. Both the Sun and Moon meet your ruler, Mars. Your secondary ruler, Pluto, also turns direct today. This is fantastic energy for you to access and use for making intentions and goals regarding your inner self. Change yourself from the inside out.

Thursday 7th

Venus leaves your sign. Make her happy by demonstrating that you have learned the value of being authentic and true to yourself. The Moon drops into your sign and your emotions verify that you're ready and committed to the hard work of self-improvement.

Friday 8th

The Sun is sitting with Mars for a few days. Determination, motivation, courage and strength are yours to arm yourself with now. This may worry a lover or close relationship and cause a few niggles. Stand up and assert your right to be authentic, but do this with a compassionate heart.

Saturday 9th

Today you can be romantic or idealistic, if just for a moment. Something will make you reminisce and put a smile on your face. Mercury backs into the Sun and Mars, and you may need to shut off and listen to your inner voice of reason and encouragement. Try not to drift away too far.

Sunday 10th

Saturn turns direct. This is good news, as the teacher planet brings tough lessons and may now dish out rewards. You should be feeling outgoing and inspired. The saying 'wind beneath my wings' will ring true for you. What will you do with this energy? Anything is possible now.

Monday 11th

Stay with the momentum and get things done. Your bank balance and home require your attention. Use that empowered energy to clean, tidy and declutter things in your home that have been neglected. Make your environment lighter and less stressful. This evening you will pull back and do more serious work.

Tuesday 12th

Today you're more methodical. You haven't run out of steam; you've simply changed your tack to look at issues that have been ongoing for a while. These could be courses of study or work projects. You may need to make a lot of phone calls or emails today. Make the most of this energy to get organised.

Wednesday 13th

When the Moon meets Pluto, you have the power to bring something to closure. Maybe a project is complete, a deal has been signed or you scrap an idea that has not worked out. Venus and Saturn help you to look at what brings you joy or not. Use this to give yourself a stronger direction.

Thursday 14th

When the Moon meets Saturn in your family sector, you may need to step up and take charge. It's your turn to be firm and fair and lead by example now. No thinking outside the box today, as that will cause further problems. Everyone must play by the rules. Lead by example.

Friday 15th

You get a bonus from the Sun in your social sector. Family life and wider groups can combine to make innovative decisions. Jupiter is involved, so expect this to be big. People are expecting the deeper truth to bring them joy. Try not to disappoint them.

Saturday 16th

Take the opportunity to use the weekend for romance or art. Today's energy brings you more inspiration, but this time you can use it to connect, be spiritual and express yourself. You may have a moment of crisis, but this can be used as a trigger or a catalyst to create something grand.

Sunday 17th

Jupiter turns direct today in your family sector. More pressure is lifted and you should experience an injection of optimism. Listening to your inner voices is important, as you'll get a feel of the direction in which you are meant to go. Many planets are supporting your growth right now.

Monday 18th

Mercury also turns direct now. He hasn't finished diving around in your psyche, although he will now clear away the debris and should give you some clarity. This afternoon you're fired up to get on with mundane jobs, and catch up people you may have neglected recently. Check on your health now, too.

Tuesday 19th

The Moon sits opposite Mercury. You may get an emotional tug which causes you to start making plans. Get out your planner and make a vision board. What new things would you like to initiate? This could be huge, seeing as Jupiter and Mars are involved. You should realise that nothing is beyond your means at this stage.

Wednesday 20th

This afternoon, a Full Moon in your health and duties sector shows you where projects, concepts or habits have been forever changed. You may feel some regret, but there are also things to celebrate. You should look at your achievements this year. By evening, you should rest as this energy can be draining.

Thursday 21st

The Moon's monthly visit to your relationship sector meets Uranus but squares off with Saturn. This can be troublesome, as Uranus disrupts the status quo and Saturn is restrictive. Try to use this energy to brainstorm new ways of relating and bring in some excitement to your relationships.

Friday 22nd

Your rulers aren't playing nicely. There may be much to do, and you must stay in control. However, energy from Mars is in your hidden sector and you may wish to use it for your own purposes. You will need to balance both and see to your duties first.

Saturday 23rd

The Sun enters your sign, signalling the arrival of your birthday month. Happy birthday. Your mind is probably extra busy now, thinking and communicating about the deeper issues of life. Philosophical concepts may fill your head. You must listen to dream messages or wisdom from elders today.

Sunday 24th

The Moon and Venus are facing each other. Venus is ready for an adventure, but the Moon is undecided. This is a great time to interact with others and get your intellectual juices flowing.

Monday 25th

You're uplifted and should feel ready for the working week. There's no time to be dragged off-course by Neptune, try to stay focused and optimistic. Serious discussions can stimulate your tastes for the bizarre or taboo today; you may delve deeper than before and find that you enjoy it.

Tuesday 26th

The Moon in your travel sector is always a little tricky. There's a nagging urge to expand your borders, which actually makes you do the opposite. This is more to do with taking a financial risk and your fears of instability. Take it one step at a time.

Wednesday 27th

Uncomfortable energy can make you feel manipulated or the victim of passive-aggression. The sensitive Moon sits opposite Pluto, who likes to be in control. Mercury is squaring off with the Moon, so you may have some reservations about working on your unconscious material. There's a strong chance that you fear being exposed in some way.

Thursday 28th

This morning you find your courage again and hold your head high. Venus and Jupiter, the two luck-bringers, are helping you to achieve harmony to family situations and your own self-worth. This influence may also bring financial gain. Do your job with true conviction and you will be noticed.

Friday 29th

Today you face Mercury's findings in your hidden sector. This may cause some problems with a lover or an important person. Alternatively, it could also shake things up to a point which has been long overdue. Pressure released from this area of life will leave space to breathe.

Saturday 30th

Exerting your will over another isn't a good idea, as Saturn is watching how you treat people. Mars has come to your sign, so expect to experience some fireworks. An ending and a new beginning are possible. Keep a level head if you can, as this has the potential to be an explosive time.

Sunday 31st

With the Moon in your social sector, you may wish for a peaceful time with close friends. You may be spontaneous and call up someone for a meet up. The Moon and Sun are in a good connection; use this energy to have light-hearted fun today.

NOVEMBER
· · · · · · · · · · · · · · · ·

Monday 1st

The Moon drops into your hidden sector. You may become
reserved and introspective now. This is the time of the month
where you find that your inner voices tend to speak to you the
most. You process recent feelings and try to justify your own
behaviour patterns. Some of these are no longer helpful to you.

Tuesday 2nd

You might feel that you're having a hard time, as Mercury
and Pluto are squaring off. Pluto asks for permanent change
and Mercury is trying to communicate this to you. This may
also manifest externally as projects you have been working
on. Responsibilities and adult duties are questioned now.
What can you release?

Wednesday 3rd

The Moon sits with Mercury. Your head and heart are having
a conversation and doing more justifying than usual. Don't
make any decisions just yet. Listen to both sides and wait until
you have clarity or ask for help. You may not have all the facts
at the moment.

Thursday 4th

This is a promising day for opportunity, as you have a New
Moon in your sign. Having just passed your ruler and opposing
Uranus, you may feel something is getting ready to explode in
your face. This is your big chance to set intentions regarding
yourself and only yourself.

Friday 5th

Venus moves into your communications sector. Here, she will mediate and research anything you wish to learn. Mercury is at the final degree of your hidden sector; it is imperative now that you ensure you have received his message and are ready for the next steps in your self-improvement plan.

Saturday 6th

Mercury and Venus are in talks today. Do you have any questions or avenues you wish to explore? Your communication skills will be honest, direct and compassionate. Consider courses of study or work advancements and how you can set these in progress. You're ready to widen your world just a little.

Sunday 7th

A fiery Moon placement in your finance and worth sector gets you to look at what you value the most. This may be beauty, connection, hard work or money. Don't let Neptune drag you into unrealistic thinking; be honest with yourself and keep it real.

Monday 8th

This is a lovely day for being authentic and communicating your desires. Venus greets the Moon and women's wisdom is highlighted. Time spent with teachers and guides will fill your soul and inspire you to follow a strong sense of direction. You could surprise yourself and a lover with how innovative you can be.

Tuesday 9th

The Moon meets Pluto in your communications sector. You have
the emotional strength to deal with any changes today. Indeed,
you may be making some of your own. Looking at things from
a different perspective is helpful. Get creative around solving a
problem and working towards a goal.

Wednesday 10th

Family time will always bring out the individual in you.
You can impress others who may underestimate just how
important your unique nature is. Mercury and Mars join
forces in your sign, and you say what you mean and mean
what you say. You're powerful today.

Thursday 11th

Big emotions are evident in your family sector. This could
cause some upset, as Uranus is connecting to this too. You
may need to shake someone out of old energy patterns and
make them wake up to the present time. They might see
you as being rebellious, but you are revolutionary.

Friday 12th

The Moon drops into your beautiful creative sector. You're able
to express yourself through art, poetry or love. This lovely energy
opens you up to connect with divine sources or simply your
higher self. Don't hold back; this is good for you.

Saturday 13th

You're on a roll and must keep up the momentum. Mercury
and Mars in your sign are both powerful allies, right now.
Use them to help you stay focused and ask for what you want.
When the Moon meets Neptune, you are dreamy; remember to
keep one foot on the ground.

Sunday 14th

You stay in the poetic zone until this afternoon, when your thoughts become more rational. You're highly motivated and desire to get on with things. Last minute weekend duties may be rushed but you should be satisfied that nothing has been neglected. Protect your energy and check your health today.

Monday 15th

Difficult energy between the Sun and Jupiter may feel like a clash of egos between yourself and a person in authority. You may fall out of favour but, as Saturn is involved, you will ultimately do the right thing. Don't take it personally, stay responsible and well behaved.

Tuesday 16th

Communications are strained today. Pluto is attached to both the Moon and the Sun. Your ego is delighted, as you're in control of an awkward conversation, but deep down your emotions are struggling with it. You may suffer a sleepless night because of this, as you're likely to dwell on it.

Wednesday 17th

This is another tricky day when you must think twice about your reactions and responses. Mars, the planet of war, is opposite Uranus, the planet of disruption. This occurs over the difficult sectors of self and others. You will feel this in your important relationships. Be mindful and practise the pause before responding.

Thursday 18th

The best thing you can do today is to stay home and hide under the duvet. There's a lot of tension in the air, which is directly affecting your confidence to relate well. You just cannot say the right thing. It's best that you lie low until this passing moon phase is over.

Friday 19th

The Full Moon in your opposite sign is the reason for this trying time. What has come to light regarding your relationships? Change has happened or is imminent. There's nothing you can do now, except to accept that this is necessary.

Saturday 20th

You may feel some relief as the Moon shifts, but your mind will be busy. You must process recent events and try to emotionally detach. Step back from the drama and let your thoughts and emotions unfold naturally. This isn't a process you can rush, so let it run its course and try to accept it for what it is.

Sunday 21st

You're not getting any closer to working out how you feel right now. The Moon holds your emotions firmly in the sector of intimacy and deep enquiry. It's up to you to learn to be rational and non-judgemental, and that includes not judging yourself. Stay logical for the moment.

Monday 22nd

Today the Moon shifts into your travel sector. You desire to stay home and be nurtured. Lick your wounds and allow another to take care of you now. Stay protected in your comfort zone and let your inner child be soothed by a maternal figure who is wise and intuitive.

Tuesday 23rd

The Moon and Venus are facing each other. You must look at the roles of mother, father, inheritance and legacy. What does all this mean to you? It may mean that you have to deal with past conditioning and adjust it to adult life. Other gentle energy will help you do this.

Wednesday 24th

Mercury is at the final degree of your sign, and asks that you mull over recent hurts before he moves. The Sun is already in your finance and value sector, which indicates that you may get a new lease of life for your home or a boost in finances. Be bold as you move forward.

Thursday 25th

A strong Moon in your career sector gets you back on your feet to deal with adulting and responsibility. Mars in your sign is connecting well to Venus, which can signify a reconciliation or simply getting what you desire. Step up and ask for something, a pay rise even. Just don't be greedy.

Friday 26th

The fiery Moon opposes Jupiter today. You may find that a person in authority will challenge you. Speak your truth, for Jupiter can represent the law and changing fortunes. Deeper truths are waiting to be discovered, so set your sights on them. Move forward on the path you are destined for.

Saturday 27th

Your heart and head may not be in sync today. Connect with your wider social groups who may be able to help you get some clarity. Question everything today and make an informed decision if one is required. Try to keep your emotions out of anything important and be open and ready to receive good advice.

Sunday 28th

If you listen well, you may be surprised at what you hear. This will concern your friendships and relationship, and will be beneficial in the long run. You will need to be grounded today as, when the Moon opposes Neptune, you will be in danger of misrepresentation.

Monday 29th

Mercury is in the heat of the Sun and asks that you listen to everything today. Dreams, messages, gossip and guidance will all help you at a later date. The Moon is back in your hidden sector, where you make discernments about recent events and people you have encountered.

Tuesday 30th

Saturn is the biggest influence on you today. This firm but fair teacher is asking you to show how responsible you are. Your finances and value system will be questioned. Look around you and see what, in your home, is keeping you small. Can you let it go now?

DECEMBER

· · · · · · · · · · · · · · · · · · ·

Wednesday 1st

Neptune turns direct. You will now see issues regarding your creative sector in a clear light. The time has come to use your muse and put your romantic and artistic endeavours to work. The Moon drops into your sign and you become empowered. Follow your passions.

Thursday 2nd

Although the Moon is opposite Uranus, you can use this energy to create positive sparks in your relationships. You're supported by Neptune and Venus. Put your heart and soul into a long-term project. Remember to abide by the rules of etiquette and you won't go wrong.

Friday 3rd

The Moon meets your ruler today in your sign. Your personal energy and drive will have an emotional attachment. It's possible that you clash with a leader or elder in the family. Be respectful but don't keep yourself small. There is more to let go of now. You're moving on.

Saturday 4th

Today there's a New Moon in your finance and values sector. You may have a goal or intention that you think is wildly unattainable. Don't discard it. Have a talk with your inner self and, if this is truly worth your while, then reach for it.

Sunday 5th

You are outgoing and upbeat today. An air of optimism surrounds you and others are attracted to it. Checking your finances and starting a savings pot is a good idea now, as Jupiter is involved here and he expands all he touches. This afternoon there may be visits or messages to attend to.

Monday 6th

There's useful energy for getting things done. Communication with lovers such as sharing your dreams will prove fruitful. Both of your rulers are working together to make you assertive, productive and goal orientated. Try catching up on work or projects you have neglected.

Tuesday 7th

The Moon meets Pluto today and also connects to Mars. Your personal energy is ongoing. You will see something come to completion now, or you may even scrap a project that has become a burden. Your family of origin may have a get-together or some news for you today.

Wednesday 8th

Stern words within your family are possible now. You may see a battle of wills where someone has to back down to keep the peace. Tension will only be released if there's respect and healthy boundaries. Mars connecting to Jupiter may blow tempers out of proportion. Deal with the fall-out when you're calmer.

Thursday 9th

Sometimes, it's better to keep the peace than to speak your truth. Today is one of those days. You will not get anywhere by being your usual, intense self. If there's drama around you, walk away and don't rise to it. Stay in a neutral place for now.

Friday 10th

Today is much quieter. The Moon has moved into your creative sector. If you need to say your piece, do it with art, poetry or music. This is a much safer way of using the unpredictable energy coming from Uranus today. You have an impulse to create and love.

Saturday 11th

You may get lost in a daydream or in your art. The muse is strong in you right now and you're urged to begin a long term or difficult project. Venus meets Pluto, making this into beautiful, transforming energy. Neptune lets your emotions drift without a care. Take this chance to allow yourself to be emotionally and creatively free.

Sunday 12th

Venus and Pluto are discussing endings, beginnings and new cycles of life. They are in your communications sector, so prepare for serious discussions about recycling something old. The Moon in your health and duties sector is eager to please and work through a checklist. Keep it real and attainable.

Monday 13th

Two planets shift signs. Mercury enters your communications sector. Expect a lot of business lunches and brainstorming now. Mars storms into your finances and value sector. Put your energy into making money and creating a home to be proud of. You can be ruthless with decluttering.

Tuesday 14th

Sweet talking over a candle-lit dinner with a lover is on the menu today. Earth energy from the Moon and Mercury provide you with an opportunity to make solid plans together. You will stay grounded and be practical. Enjoy the delights of a tasty meal or get sensual.

Wednesday 15th

The Moon meets Uranus and you may feel the Earth move today. The combination of emotions and instability can go two different ways today. Stay mindful, as you may experience volatile feelings bubbling up. This energy can also manifest as positive electrical charges and fireworks. Maybe it's time to celebrate the season early?

Thursday 16th

Today is also filled with good energy for lovers or self-care. Neptune connects and shows you what is possible in a relationship when you look through the eyes of the other. Venus and Pluto ask you to look at making or recreating something beautiful. Work at finding the hidden gold.

Friday 17th

You have a mini-crisis today, which may involve money. The festive season can be expensive and today you may feel that your money is being leaked out in all directions. Check on finances you share with another or on other investments. Maybe you can pull some back in now.

Saturday 18th

Venus turns retrograde tonight. She will turn away from Pluto and retrace her steps in your communications sector for several weeks. Recycling projects will be on hold now. You may see the return of an old lover or have a new interest in a project you have previously discarded.

Sunday 19th

A Full Moon in your intimacy sector will illuminate where your mind is busy with enquiry. You may have been researching a deep and intense subject and can now grasp the concept of it. This moon may also help to settle an indecision or two. Late morning the Moon shifts and you crave security.

Monday 20th

Your head and emotions do battle today. It's possible that your to-do list is so long that you cannot face it. This is harmless and is only you reacting to feeling a little overwhelmed. If you need to have a meltdown, punch some pillows. Then sleep on them.

Tuesday 21st

The Winters Solstice ushers the Sun into your communications sector. Give yourself time to pause in this busy period. Reflect on the year gone by and contemplate how much has changed. The longest night will bring you dreams and messages, so listen carefully. Trust your intuition now.

Wednesday 22nd

The Moon is now in your courageous career sector, but this is no time to stand out from the crowd. Join in the festive fun but remember to play by the rules. Family needs are important now, too. You may have to decline an invitation to the office party as you have duties to attend to.

Thursday 23rd

Today is an auspicious time of stillness from the planets. Jupiter is at the final degree of your family sector. This is a clear statement about where you should be now. Share the joy of the season with your nearest and dearest. Let your unique light shine.

Friday 24th

Social invitations from your wider groups come in, but you're obliged to consider where you are needed most. Think carefully as the more disruptive planets are connecting and tension is building. Be of service today and do your best to co-operate. Tempers may flare in the evening.

Saturday 25th

The celebrations are here, and the planetary connections suggest a level of high activity and chatter. Sacrifices may need to be made of your time. Venus retrograde bumps into Pluto today. Watch out for subtle manipulation tactics or passive-aggression. Be prepared to help out and encourage others to do the same so that all the work doesn't fall on the same person or people.

Sunday 26th

You have managed to survive a day that some people find testing. Venus and Pluto both connect well to the Moon today and you should feel emotionally stable. Take some time this evening to unwind, detach from others and process your thoughts alone. Listen to your dreams tonight.

Monday 27th

Today is reasonably quiet. Your energy returns with some help from your ruler. It is possible that you act as a go-between or you are asked for wise judgement on a matter. You are good at seeing both sides of an issue and others come to you for that.

Tuesday 28th

You need time alone or with a very select group. The Moon is in your hidden sector but squares off with planets that can cause you unrest. Your mind will be full from the last few days and you may judge yourself too harshly. Try to find the value somehow.

Wednesday 29th

The Moon is in your sign. Of course, the monthly opposition to Uranus can be unsettling but you must work it to your advantage. Have a lively, fun time with a partner. Jupiter enters your creative sector for the next twelve months. This is highly beneficial; lucky you.

Thursday 30th

Mercury and Pluto meet up today in your communications sector. You may talk yourself into taking on a huge new project or ending one now. This is a day where you can dream big and put your own self first above everything else. Self-care is essential now; remember that Venus taught you that.

Friday 31st

The end of the year sees the Moon meet the point of past karma and also Mars. This occurs in your finance and values sector. You know what did not work this year, now forget it and march on. Enjoy the celebrations with your head held high.

Scorpio

·················

PEOPLE WHO SHARE
YOUR SIGN

PEOPLE WHO SHARE YOUR SIGN

....

Scorpios have seduced our screens for decades, from Scarlett Johansson to Goldie Hawn, so it's no wonder that they have a reputation for being the sexiest sign in the zodiac calendar. The Scorpion is a mysterious creature that has brought dark depths to the world in the form of Martin Scorsese's films of the macabre and transformational wonders in the form of RuPaul's Drag Race. Discover which of these intriguing Scorpios share your exact birthday and see if you can spot the similarities.

24th October
Shenae Grimes (1989), Eliza Taylor (1989), Drake (1986), Wayne Rooney (1985), Katie McGrath (1983), Roman Abramovich (1966), Malcolm Turnbull, Australian Prime Minister (1954), Kevin Kline (1947)

25th October
Rylan Clark-Neal (1988), Ciara (1985), Katy Perry (1984), Craig Robinson (1971), David Furnish (1962), Chad Smith (1961), Pablo Picasso (1881), Johann Strauss II (1825)

26th October
Seth MacFarlane (1973), Phaedra Parks (1973), Tom Cavanagh (1968), Keith Urban (1967), Uhuru Kenyatta, Kenyan President (1961), Dylan McDermott (1961), Rita Wilson (1956), Hillary Clinton (1947), Jaclyn Smith (1945)

27th October
Kelly Osbourne (1984), Marla Maples (1963), Simon Le Bon (1958), Luiz Inácio Lula da Silva, Brazilian President (1945), John Cleese (1939), Sylvia Plath (1932), Roy Lichtenstein (1923), Theodore Roosevelt, U.S. President (1858)

28th October
Frank Ocean (1987), Troian Bellisario (1985), Matt Smith (1982), Joaquin Phoenix (1974), Julia Roberts (1967), Matt Drudge (1966), Bill Gates (1955), Caitlyn Jenner (1949)

29th October
Tove Lo (1987), Ben Foster (1980), Tracee Ellis Ross (1972), Gabrielle Union (1972), Winona Ryder (1971), Rufus Sewell (1967), Kate Jackson (1948), Richard Dreyfuss (1947)

30th October
Janel Parrish (1988), Clémence Poésy (1982), Ivanka Trump (1981), Matthew Morrison (1978), Nia Long (1970), Gavin Rossdale (1965), Diego Maradona (1960), Timothy B. Schmit (1947), Henry Winkler (1945)

31st October
Willow Smith (2000), Frank Iero (1981), Piper Perabo (1976),Vanilla Ice (1967), Rob Schneider (1963), Peter Jackson (1961), John Candy (1950), Zaha Hadid (1950), Michael Landon (1936), Carlos Drummond de Andrade (1902), Sardar Patel (1875)

1st November

Penn Badgley (1986), Aishwarya Rai (1973), Jenny McCarthy (1972), Jeremy Hunt (1966), Anthony Kiedis (1962), Tim Cook (1960), David Foster (1949), Larry Flynt (1942)

2nd November

Nelly (1974), Stevie J (1971), David Schwimmer (1966), Shahrukh Khan (1965), Warren G. Harding, U.S. President (1865), James Knox Polk, U.S. President (1795), Marie Antionette (1755)

3rd November

Kendall Jenner (1995), Colin Kaepernick (1987), Gabe Newell (1962), Dolph Lundgren (1957), Kate Capshaw (1953), Larry Holmes (1949), Anna Wintour (1949)

4th November

Jessa Seewald (1992), Dez Bryant (1988), Guy Martin (1981), Bethenny Frankel (1970), P. Diddy (1969), Matthew McConaughey (1969), Ralph Macchio (1961), Kathy Griffin (1960)

5th November

Virat Kohli (1988), Kevin Jonas (1987), Alexa Chung (1983), Luke Hemsworth (1981), Danniella Westbrook (1973), Famke Janssen (1964), Tilda Swinton (1960), Bryan Adams (1959), Kris Jenner (1955)

6th November

Kris Wu (1990), Emma Stone (1988), Conchita Wurst (1988), Taryn Manning (1978), Thandie Newton (1972), Rebecca Romijn (1972), Ethan Hawke (1970), Kelly Rutherford (1968), Mohamed Hadid (1948), Sally Field (1946)

7th November

Lorde (1996), Bethany Mota (1995), David de Gea (1990), Elsa Hosk (1988), David Guetta (1967), Joni Mitchell (1943), Albert Camus (1913), Marie Curie (1867)

8th November

Jasmine Thompson (2000), Lauren Alaina (1994), Jessica Lowndes (1988), Erica Mena (1987) Tara Reid (1975), Tech N9ne (1971), Gordon Ramsay (1966), Bonnie Raitt (1949), Alain Delon (1935)

9th November

French Montana (1984), Caroline Flack (1979), Nick Lachey (1973), Eric Dane (1972), Lou Ferrigno (1951), Carl Sagan (1934), Hedy Lamarr (1914), Muhammad Iqbal (1877)

10th November

Mackenzie Foy (2000), Kiernan Shipka (1999), Zoey Deutch (1994), Taron Egerton (1989), Josh Peck (1986), Miranda Lambert (1983), Diplo (1978), Eve (1978), Brittany Murphy (1977), Ellen Pompeo (1969), Hugh Bonneville (1963), Neil Gaiman (1960)

11th November

Tye Sheridan (1996), Vinny Guadagnino (1987), Philipp Lahm (1983), Leonardo DiCaprio (1974), Calista Flockhart (1964), Demi Moore (1962), Stanley Tucci (1960), Kurt Vonnegut (1922), Fyodor Dostoevsky (1821)

12th November

Anne Hathaway (1982), Ryan Gosling (1980), Gustaf Skarsgård (1980), Tonya Harding (1970), Nadia Comăneci (1961), Megan Mullally (1958), Hassan Rouhani, Iranian President (1948), Neil Young (1945), Grace Kelly (1929)

13th November

Matt Bennett (1991), Devon Bostick (1991), Gerard Butler (1969), Jimmy Kimmel (1967), Steve Zahn (1967), Whoopi Goldberg (1955), Chris Noth (1954), Frances Conroy (1953), Andrés Manuel López Obrador, Mexican President-elect (1953), Robert Louis Stevenson (1850)

14th November

Russell Tovey (1981), Olga Kurylenko (1979), Travis Barker (1975), Gary Vaynerchuk (1975), Josh Duhamel (1972), Patrick Warburton (1964), Charles, Prince of Wales (1948), Astrid Lindgren (1907), Claude Monet (1840)

15th November

Paulo Dybala (1993), Shailene Woodley (1991), B.o.B (1988), Sania Mirza (1986), Lily Aldridge (1985), Jeffree Star (1985), Chad Kroeger (1974), Jonny Lee Miller (1972), Jimmy Choo (1948)

16th November

Pete Davidson (1993), Vicky Pattison (1987), Gemma Atkinson (1984), Maggie Gyllenhaal (1977), Paul Scholes (1974), Brandi Glanville (1972), Missi Pyle (1972), Lisa Bonet (1967), Sheree Zampino (1967)

17th November

Tom Ellis (1978), Rachel McAdams (1978), Lorraine Pascale (1972), Jeff Buckley (1966), Jonathan Ross (1960), RuPaul (1960), Danny DeVito (1944), Lauren Hutton (1943), Martin Scorsese (1942)

18th November

Nick Bateman (1986), Fabolous (1977), Anthony McPartlin (1975), Chloë Sevigny (1974), Owen Wilson (1968), Kirk Hammett (1962), Elizabeth Perkins (1960), Kim Wilde (1960), Linda Evans (1942)

19th November

Tyga (1989), Adam Driver (1983), Jack Dorsey (1976), Jodie Foster (1962), Meg Ryan (1961), Allison Janney (1959), Charlie Kaufman (1958), Calvin Klein (1942), Larry King (1933), Indira Gandhi, Indian Prime Minister (1917)

20th November

Michael Clifford (1995), Oliver Sykes (1986), Future (1983), Andrea Riseborough (1981), Kimberley Walsh (1981), Ming-Na Wen (1963), Sean Young (1959), Bo Derek (1956), Joe Walsh (1947)

21st November

Conor Maynard (1992), Colleen Ballinger (1986), Carly Rae Jepsen (1985), Jena Malone (1984), Nikki Bella (1983), Ken Block (1967), Björk (1965), Nicollette Sheridan (1963), Goldie Hawn (1945), René Magritte (1898)

22nd November

Hailey Baldwin (1996), Alden Ehrenreich (1989), Scarlett Johansson (1984), Boris Becker (1967), Mark Ruffalo (1967), Mads Mikkelsen (1965), Jamie Lee Curtis (1958), Rodney Dangerfield (1921)